# ★ contents

WeightWatchers®

# meals in minutes

## 150
### SPEEDY RECIPES
### LOW IN
### *POINTS*® VALUES

WEIGHT WATCHERS
PUBLISHING GROUP

Creative and Editorial Director
**Nancy Gagliardi**

Art Director
**Ed Melnitsky**

Production Manager
**Alan Biederman**

Office Manager/
Publishing Assistant
**Jenny Laboy-Brace**

Food Editor
**Carol Prager**

Photographers
**Rita Maas**
**Ann Stratton**

Designers
**Julia Michry**
**Carol Pagliuco**

Consulting Editor
**Barbara Turvett**

# A Word About Weight Watchers

Since 1963, Weight Watchers has grown from a handful of people to millions of enrollments annually. Today, Weight Watchers is recognized as the leading name in safe and sensible weight control. Weight Watchers members form a diverse group, from youths to senior citizens, attending meetings virtually around the globe. Weight-loss and weight-management results vary by individual, but we recommend that you attend Weight Watchers meetings, follow the Weight Watchers food plan, and participate in regular physical activity. For a Weight Watchers meeting near you, call 800-651-6000. Also, check out *Weight Watchers* Magazine (for subscription information call 800-978-2400) and visit us at our Web site: WeightWatchers.com.

## Icons

🔥 hot/spicy

🚫 no cooking

🍳 one pot

🕐 20 minutes or less

🥕 vegetarian

# Introduction

★ ★ ★ ★ ★ ★ ★ ★ ★ ★ ★ ★ ★ ★ ★ ★ ★ ★ ★ ★ ★ ★ ★ ★ ★ ★ ★ ★ ★ ★ ★ ★ ★ ★ ★

When I think about hearty, homemade meals, the image that comes to mind is a huge pot perched on the stove early on a Sunday morning. Inside was the sauce—a heady mix of fresh tomatoes laced with chopped basil, garlic, pork, and meatballs that simmered, untouched (except for the occasional stir), for hours. That fragrant, mouth-watering mix with its intense tomatoey taste would be the heart of countless Sunday dinners—and set the bar high for what home cooking tastes like in my mind.

What dishes make up *your* childhood memories? Classic answers to this question might include meatloaf, fried chicken, macaroni and cheese, mashed potatoes, and chocolate cake. But in a changing world, things aren't quite so straightforward anymore. Ask this question in America today and you'll likely get a diverse lot of responses: Jamaican jerk chicken (think hot and spicy), Polish perogies (doughy pillows stuffed with everything from meat to cheese), Asian congee (a creamy, soupy breakfast of boiled rice and water laced with meats), Puerto Rican fried plantains (firm, starchy bananas), Irish colcannon (a mix of mashed potatoes with onions and cabbage), Indian curries (spicy or savory meat or vegetables—or both—stews), and the list goes on.

Yet even as our culinary tastes continue to grow and change to mirror the marvelous melting pot of this country, the way we choose to prepare meals has evolved, as well. Our melting-pot society is also a fast-moving one, so we want great food on the table—quickly. That's why we've created this new collection of recipes.

*Weight Watchers Meals in Minutes: 150 Speedy Recipes Low in* **POINTS** *Values* includes what we consider to be the quick new classics you'll make over and over for your family and friends. And while the recipes are diverse, all were created with some common threads: They're easy on the cook, they're **POINTS** value conscious, and they boast a bold and tantalizing blend of flavors.

So shake up your eating routine, try a recipe or two, and discover some user-friendly new classics you'll make and savor for years to come.

Regards,

Nancy Gagliardi

Creative and Editorial Director

★ ★ ★ ★ ★ ★ ★ ★ ★ ★ ★ ★ ★ ★ ★ ★ ★ ★ ★ ★ ★ ★ ★ ★ ★ ★ ★ ★ ★ ★ ★ ★ ★ ★ ★

# CHAPTER 1

# what's for breakfast?

### FILLING AND DELICIOUS MORNING MEALS TO KEEP YOU GOING LIKE A CHAMPION

# Honey-Ginger Fruit Compote

**MAKES 6 SERVINGS**

Try your own favorite fruit combination in this simple, refreshing compote. Chopping the crystallized ginger with the sour cream in a food processor or blender serves to aerate the sour cream; for a denser topping, chop the ginger by hand and whisk it into the sour cream. Plain fat-free yogurt can be substituted for the sour cream, if you prefer.

$^2/_3$ **cup reduced-fat
   sour cream**
$2^1/_2$ **tablespoons chopped
   crystallized ginger**
1 **Valencia orange,
   sectioned and seeded**
$^1/_2$ **pound fresh strawberries,
   hulled and quartered**
$^1/_2$ **pint fresh blueberries**
$^1/_2$ **pint fresh raspberries**
$^1/_4$ **cup orange liqueur**

**1.** Combine the sour cream and crystallized ginger in a food processor or blender and chop until the ginger reaches a fine consistency.

**2.** Mix together the orange, strawberries, blueberries, and raspberries in a bowl. Stir in the liqueur. Serve topped with the ginger cream.

Per serving ($^2/_3$ cup compote with about 2 tablespoons ginger cream): 122 Cal, 3 g Fat, 2 g Sat Fat, 9 mg Chol, 23 mg Sod, 18 g Carb, 3 g Fib, 3 g Prot, 68 mg Calc. *POINTS* value: *2.*

**COOK TO COOK** This makes a lovely dessert, too. If you prefer to avoid alcohol, use orange juice instead of the liqueur.

meals in minutes

# Bacon Biscuits

**MAKES 16 SERVINGS**

These old-fashioned Southern-style biscuits are dropped, not rolled. Although using a ¼-cup measure or large spoon and a sharp snap of the wrist is one way to drop the dough onto the baking sheet, a 2-inch ice cream scoop with a spring-release handle is easier.

2 cups all-purpose flour

2½ teaspoons baking powder

½ teaspoon salt

⅛ teaspoon baking soda

3 tablespoons cold unsalted butter, cut into bits

4 strips crisp-cooked turkey bacon, chopped

1 cup low-fat buttermilk

¼ cup fat-free milk

1. Preheat the oven to 425°F. Spray a 9-inch round cake pan with nonstick spray.

2. In a large bowl, whisk together the flour, baking powder, salt, and baking soda. With a pastry blender or a large fork, cut in the butter to coarse crumbs. Stir in the bacon. Mix in the buttermilk and milk to form a dough.

3. Drop the dough by ¼-cup measures into the pan, making 16 mounds; push the mounds together. Bake until golden, about 20 minutes. Serve at once.

Per serving (1 biscuit): 92 Cal, 3 g Fat, 2 g Sat Fat, 9 mg Chol, 183 mg Sod, 13 g Carb, 0 g Fib, 3 g Prot, 27 mg Calc. **POINTS** value: **2.**

For best results, bake the turkey bacon in a 425°F oven until brown and very crispy, 12–15 minutes. Chop it after cooking.

# Stuffed French Toast

**MAKES 4 SERVINGS**

Baking rather than griddling the toast saves steps, pares fat, and eliminates mess—and it produces crisper French toast. Start with a whole loaf of rich egg bread and cut it yourself into ½-inch-thick slices.

⅓ cup dried cherries
1 tablespoon golden rum
8 slices challah or other egg bread
1 tablespoon chopped almonds
1 large egg
2 egg whites
¼ cup low-fat buttermilk
1 teaspoon confectioners' sugar

1. Combine the cherries and rum in a small bowl. Let the mixture soak for 10 minutes.

2. Place a heavy-gauge nonstick baking sheet in the oven and preheat the oven to 400°F. Lay 4 slices of the bread on a large plate. Mix the almonds with the cherries and rum, then scatter 2 tablespoons of the mixture over each slice. Top each with a second slice of bread. In a small bowl, beat the egg with the egg whites and buttermilk. Pour over the stuffed toast and turn the toast over to coat evenly. Let stand 10 minutes, then press the edges down to seal.

3. Spray the heated baking sheet with nonstick spray. Transfer the stuffed toast to the baking sheet and bake 10 minutes, then turn the toast over and bake until well browned and bubbling, 6–7 minutes longer. Dust with confectioners' sugar before serving.

Per serving (1 stuffed toast): 327 Cal, 7 g Fat, 2 g Sat Fat, 95 mg Chol, 455 mg Sod, 49 g Carb, 3 g Fib, 13 g Prot, 110 mg Calc.
**POINTS** value: **7.**

Use either sweet or tart dried cherries, as you prefer, or substitute an equal amount of dried cranberries, raisins, sliced fresh banana, or fresh blueberries.

meals in minutes

# Peppery Popovers

**MAKES 8 SERVINGS**

Popovers, puffy mini breads with a crisp brown crust and a tender, moist interior, are said to have gotten their name from the fact that as the batter bakes and expands, it "pops over" the sides of the cup-shaped pan. This dough is very wet. When heated, the moisture turns into steam, which causes a spectacular rise. Take care not to open the oven door while the popovers bake, as this will allow the steam that makes them rise to escape.

2 **large eggs**
1 **cup fat-free milk**
1 **cup all-purpose flour**
1/2 **teaspoon salt**
1/4 **teaspoon freshly ground pepper**

**1.** Preheat oven to 450°F. Spray 8 cups of a popover pan or muffin tin with nonstick spray.

**2.** In a medium bowl, with an electric mixer on medium speed, beat the eggs until frothy. Beat in the milk, then the flour, salt, and pepper. Spoon 1/4 cup of the batter into each cup. Bake 15 minutes; reduce the oven temperature to 400°F and bake until browned, about 12 minutes longer. Serve at once.

Per serving (1 popover): 85 Cal, 1 g Fat, 0 g Sat Fat, 47 mg Chol, 176 mg Sod, 14 g Carb, 0 g Fib, 4 g Prot, 46 mg Calc. *POINTS* value: *2.*

Use popover pans or single-weight muffin tins. Don't use insulated tins; they won't get hot enough to generate sufficient steam.

COOK TO COOK

meals in minutes

# Morning Glory Muffins

**MAKES 18 SERVINGS**

Be sure to use old-fashioned rolled oats in this recipe. Steel-cut Irish oats require more moisture and take longer to cook, and quick-cooking or instant oats would give the muffins a pasty texture.

1 **cup raisins**
$^2/_3$ **cup boiling water**
$1^3/_4$ **cup all-purpose flour**
$1^1/_4$ **cups old-fashioned rolled oats**
$^1/_4$ **cup granulated sugar**
$2^1/_2$ **teaspoons baking powder**
1 **teaspoon cinnamon**
$^1/_2$ **teaspoon salt**
2 **large eggs**
1 **cup low-fat buttermilk**
$^3/_4$ **cup packed dark brown sugar**
3 **tablespoons unsalted butter, melted**

**1.** Preheat the oven to 375°F. Spray an 18-cup muffin tin with nonstick spray. In a small bowl, combine the raisins and boiling water.

**2.** In a medium bowl, whisk the flour, oats, granulated sugar, baking powder, cinnamon, and salt. In a large bowl whisk the eggs until frothy; whisk in the buttermilk, brown sugar, and butter. Stir in the raisins and their soaking liquid. Add the flour mixture and stir to just blend (do not overmix).

**3.** Spoon the batter into the muffin cups, filling each about three-quarters full. Bake until a tester inserted into the center of a muffin comes out clean, 20–22 minutes. Remove from the pan and cool on wire racks.

Per serving (1 muffin): 169 Cal, 3 g Fat, 2 g Sat Fat, 26 mg Chol, 123 mg Sod, 33 g Carb, 1 g Fib, 4 g Prot, 37 mg Calc. **POINTS** value: **3.**

**COOK TO COOK** If you prefer a little crunch, sprinkle each muffin with about 1 teaspoon chopped pecans before baking.

# Cherry Muffins with Amaretto Glaze

**MAKES 18 SERVINGS**

Use fresh sour cherries when they're plentiful, during June and July. The rest of the year, thaw frozen sour cherries, or rinse and drain canned sour cherries. Make sure that the muffins have cooled completely before you glaze them; if you brush on the syrup while the muffins are still warm, it will be absorbed rather than harden into a topping.

- 1 cup low-fat buttermilk
- 2 large eggs
- 4 tablespoons unsalted butter, melted
- 1 teaspoon almond extract
- ½ cup packed dark brown sugar
- 1²/₃ cups all-purpose flour
- ½ tablespoon baking powder
- 1 teaspoon baking soda
- ½ teaspoon salt
- 1¼ cups fresh sour cherries, pitted
- ¼ cup granulated sugar
- ¼ cup amaretto liqueur

**1.** Preheat the oven to 375°F. Spray an 18-cup muffin tin with nonstick spray.

**2.** In a large bowl, whisk the buttermilk, eggs, butter, and almond extract. Whisk in the brown sugar. Add the flour, baking powder, baking soda, and salt; stir to combine. Fold in the sour cherries.

**3.** Spoon the batter into the muffin cups, filling each about three-quarters full. Bake until a tester inserted into the center of a muffin comes out clean, 20–22 minutes. Cool in the pan on a rack 30 minutes; remove from the pan and cool completely on the rack.

**4.** To make the glaze, in a small saucepan combine the granulated sugar and amaretto over medium heat; stir constantly until the sugar dissolves. Bring to a boil, reduce the heat to low, and simmer until a thick syrup forms, about 10 minutes. Brush over the muffins.

Per serving (1 muffin): 129 Cal, 3 g Fat, 2 g Sat Fat, 28 mg Chol, 178 mg Sod, 21 g Carb, 0 g Fib, 2 g Prot, 28 mg Calc. *POINTS* value: *3.*

When you test the muffins, make sure your toothpick or cake tester is touching the bready part of the muffin, not a cherry. Cooling the muffins in the pan allows the muffins to reabsorb the juices released by the cherries.

meals in minutes

# Hominy Focaccia

**MAKES 8 SERVINGS**

Hominy grits add a crunchy texture and a distinctly American accent to this tasty Italian treat. Be sure to use quick grits, as long-cooking grits will not soften sufficiently. Serve with a colorful fruit salad.

2¼ cups all-purpose flour
1 cup quick grits
1 envelope quick-rise yeast
1 tablespoon salt
1 egg white
1 cup lukewarm (105°F–115°F) water
1 large red onion, sliced
2 tablespoons balsamic vinegar
½ pound sweet Italian-style turkey sausage
2 teaspoons olive oil
1 teaspoon fresh thyme leaves
½ teaspoon coarsely ground black pepper
¼ teaspoon fennel seeds
⅛ teaspoon coarse salt

1. Combine the flour, grits, yeast, salt, and egg white in a food processor. Process for 1 minute, then drizzle in the water through the feed tube. After the dough forms a ball, continue to run for about 1 minute to knead.

2. Spray a large bowl with nonstick spray; put the dough in the bowl. Roll to coat the dough, cover lightly with plastic wrap, and let rise in a warm spot until it doubles in size and no longer springs back to the touch, about 30 minutes.

3. Spray a 9 x 13-inch baking pan with nonstick spray. Transfer the dough to the baking pan and press it to cover the baking pan evenly. Cover the dough loosely with plastic wrap and set aside for 15 minutes.

4. Meanwhile, preheat the oven to 425°F. Toss the onion in the vinegar and put in a baking dish. Bake until soft, about 9 minutes, stirring every 3 minutes. Brown the turkey sausage in a skillet, breaking it apart with a spoon, until crumbly and no longer pink. Drain on paper towels.

5. Push the dough flat, leaving a ½-inch raised border around the edge. Brush with the olive oil. Layer with the onion, then the sausage, and top with the thyme. Sprinkle with the pepper, fennel seeds, and coarse salt. Spray with nonstick spray. Bake until the top is lightly browned and the bread sounds hollow when tapped, about 20 minutes. Cool in the pan on a rack 10 minutes. Cut into 8 squares and serve warm or at room temperature.

Per serving (1 square): 265 Cal, 4 g Fat, 1 g Sat Fat, 15 mg Chol, 532 mg Sod, 45 g Carb, 2 g Fib, 11 g Prot, 19 mg Calc. *POINTS* value: *5.*

what's for breakfast?

Blueberry Sour Cream
Coffee Cake

# Blueberry Sour Cream Coffee Cake

**MAKES 12 SERVINGS**

Brimming with blueberries and topped with a crunchy, orange-accented streusel, this homemade coffee cake offers a delightful alternative to commercial fare. Five-spice powder, which lends this confection a distinct sweet-savory flavor, is a blend of cinnamon, cloves, star anise, fennel, and black pepper.

1 large egg
2 tablespoons canola oil
³/₄ cup granulated sugar
¹/₂ cup reduced-fat sour cream
¹/₃ cup low-fat buttermilk
2¹/₃ cups all-purpose flour
1 tablespoon baking powder
¹/₂ teaspoon five-spice powder
1¹/₂ cups fresh blueberries
¹/₄ cup packed dark brown sugar
1 teaspoon grated orange zest
2 tablespoons butter

1. Preheat the oven to 350°F. Spray a 7 x 11-inch baking dish with nonstick spray.

2. Combine the egg, oil, and granulated sugar in a bowl. Whisk until pale yellow, then whisk in the sour cream and buttermilk. In a large bowl, mix together 2 cups of the flour, the baking powder, and five-spice powder. Mix in the egg mixture. Pour the batter into the baking dish, then scatter the blueberries on top.

3. Combine the brown sugar, orange zest, butter, and the remaining ¹/₃ cup flour. Mix with the back of a fork until crumbly, then sprinkle over the batter. Bake until a tester inserted into the center of the cake comes out clean, about 45 minutes. Cool slightly, then cut into 12 pieces.

Per serving (1 piece): 225 Cal, 6 g Fat, 2 g Sat Fat, 27 mg Chol, 145 mg Sod, 40 g Carb, 1 g Fib, 4 g Prot, 101 mg Calc. **POINTS** value: **5.**

If five-spice powder isn't handy on your spice rack, use an equal amount of ground cinnamon instead.

# Goat Cheese–Stuffed Omelette

**MAKES 4 SERVINGS**  🕐

This easy entertaining breakfast entails making just one large omelette and cutting it into wedges. Choose a smooth rather than crumbly goat cheese, such as Montrachet, so that when it melts it will create a creamy filling.

1 leek, cleaned and sliced
1¼ cups chopped shiitake
   mushrooms
2 tablespoons goat cheese
1 (7-ounce) jar roasted
   red peppers, rinsed
   and drained
1 tablespoon tomato paste
¼ teaspoon coarsely ground
   black pepper
¼ teaspoon dried thyme
1 cup fat-free egg
   substitute, beaten
   until frothy

**1.** Spray a medium nonstick skillet with nonstick spray and set over high heat. Add the leek slices and cook, stirring, until they just start to brown; then add the mushrooms and cook until well browned. Transfer the vegetables to a bowl and stir in the goat cheese.

**2.** To make the sauce, puree the roasted peppers, tomato paste, pepper, and thyme in a food processor or blender.

**3.** Spray a large nonstick skillet with nonstick spray and set over medium-high heat until smoking. Pour in the egg substitute and swirl to cover the pan. Cook, stirring gently, until the underside is set, 2–3 minutes. Spread the vegetables evenly over half of the omelette; fold the other half over the filling. Slide the omelette onto a plate and pour the sauce on top. Cut into 4 wedges.

Per serving (1 wedge with ¼ of sauce): 109 Cal, 2 g Fat, 1 g Sat Fat, 4 mg Chol, 318 mg Sod, 14 g Carb, 2 g Fib, 9 g Prot, 73 mg Calc. *POINTS* value: *2.*

meals in minutes

# Puffed Egg-White Omelette with Veggies

**MAKES 4 SERVINGS**

The trick to making this filled omelette taste great is to make sure the peppers and onion are well cooked. By doing this, the liquid in the vegetables evaporates and the natural sugars are released.

2 teaspoons olive oil

1 green bell pepper, seeded and thinly sliced

1 red bell pepper, seeded and thinly sliced

1 onion, thinly sliced

½ teaspoon salt

10 egg whites, at room temperature

½ cup shredded reduced-fat cheddar cheese

1. Heat the oil in a large ovenproof nonstick skillet over medium-high heat. Add the green and red bell peppers, onion, and ¼ teaspoon of the salt and cook, stirring occasionally, until the vegetables are very tender, about 8 minutes. Slowly pour in 5 of the egg whites; sprinkle with the cheese. Cook over medium heat, stirring gently, until slightly firm, 3–5 minutes. Remove from the heat.

2. Preheat the broiler.

3. In a large bowl, with an electric mixer on high speed, beat the remaining 5 egg whites and the remaining ¼ teaspoon salt until soft peaks form, 3–4 minutes. Spoon over the vegetable mixture to cover completely. Broil 7 inches from the heat until puffed and just golden, about 5 minutes. Cut into 4 wedges and serve at once.

Per serving (1 wedge): 122 Cal, 4 g Fat, 2 g Sat Fat, 8 mg Chol, 504 mg Sod, 6 g Carb, 2 g Fib, 14 g Prot, 117 mg Calc. **POINTS** value: **2.**

When separating the eggs for this omelette, keep 5 of them in a small bowl and the remaining 5, which will be beaten separately, in large bowl.

what's for breakfast?

# Quick and Light Eggs Florentine

**MAKES 4 SERVINGS**

In this simple update of the brunch classic, the eggs and the spinach are cooked together. We also serve it in a ramekin instead of atop an English muffin. A light orange sauce replaces the typically fat-laden hollandaise.

1⅓ cups orange juice
1 tablespoon cornstarch
½ tablespoon butter
2 scallions, sliced
1 (10-ounce) box frozen chopped spinach, thawed and squeezed dry
½ teaspoon ground coriander
½ teaspoon salt
¼ teaspoon coarsely ground black pepper
4 large eggs

**1.** Preheat the oven to 350°F. Whisk together the orange juice and cornstarch in a bowl. Melt the butter in a small saucepan over medium heat. Add the scallions and cook until limp and translucent, then add the orange juice mixture and cook until the sauce is thick and clear, 6–7 minutes. Reduce heat to low to keep the sauce warm.
**2.** Combine the spinach, coriander, salt, pepper, and ½ cup of the orange sauce in a bowl. Put 3 tablespoons of the mixture into each of 4 (¾-cup) ramekins, creating wells in the centers. Break an egg into each well. Put the ramekins on a baking sheet and bake until the eggs are set, 16–17 minutes. Spoon about 2 tablespoons of the remaining sauce over each.

Per serving (1 egg Florentine with 2 tablespoons sauce): 176 Cal, 10 g Fat, 4 g Sat Fat, 224 mg Chol, 409 mg Sod, 14 g Carb, 2 g Fib, 9 g Prot, 118 mg Calc. *POINTS* value: *4.*

**COOK TO COOK** Frozen spinach is used as a convenience. If you prefer to use fresh, rinse a 10-ounce bag of triple-washed spinach, leaving some water clinging to the leaves. Then dry-sauté until well wilted, about a minute.

# Potato and Pepper Frittata

**MAKES 4 SERVINGS**

A frittata is the ultimate easy-on-the-cook egg dish for breakfast or brunch. Here, we use a classic mix of potatoes, peppers, and cheddar cheese, but you could substitute other vegetables, such as zucchini, chopped broccoli, or tomatoes, and other cheeses, such as feta or Monterey Jack.

1 tablespoon canola oil

2 cups frozen hash-brown potatoes (from a 32-ounce bag)

1 bunch scallions, thinly sliced

1 red bell pepper, seeded and chopped

³/₄ teaspoon salt

¹/₄ cup chopped flat-leaf parsley

2 cups fat-free egg substitute

¹/₂ cup shredded reduced-fat cheddar cheese

1 tablespoon shredded Parmesan cheese

¹/₂ teaspoon coarsely ground black pepper

**1.** Heat the oil in a medium nonstick skillet over medium heat. Add the hash browns, scallions, bell pepper, and salt; cook, stirring frequently, until the vegetables are tender and golden, 8–10 minutes. Stir in the parsley.

**2.** Meanwhile, spray a large nonstick skillet with nonstick spray and set over medium heat. Add the egg substitute and cook until set, 7–8 minutes, lifting the edges often with a spatula to let the uncooked egg flow underneath.

**3.** Spoon the potato mixture over the frittata, then sprinkle with the cheddar cheese, Parmesan cheese, and ground pepper. Cover the skillet and cook until the cheese melts, about 3 minutes.

Per serving (¹/₄ frittata): 190 Cal, 4 g Fat, 1 g Sat Fat, 1 mg Chol, 653 mg Sod, 26 g Carb, 4 g Fib, 13 g Prot, 98 mg Calc. **POINTS** value: **3.**

**COOK TO COOK** For a nicely browned cheese topping, pop the frittata under a hot broiler for 2 to 3 minutes after you complete step 3. If the handle on your skillet is not flameproof, cover it with heavy-duty foil.

what's for breakfast?

# Santa Fe Corn-and-Cheddar Cakes

**MAKES 4 SERVINGS**

Replacing wheat flour with masa harina yields an unusually light, soufflé-like breakfast cake. These triple-size "pancakes" (one per person makes a generous serving) are baked in ramekins rather than cooked on a griddle. They can also be served as a luncheon entrée, accompanied by a mixed green salad with a spicy dressing.

1 cup fat-free egg substitute
3 tablespoons masa harina
2/3 cup low-fat buttermilk
1 tablespoon butter, melted
1/2 teaspoon salt
Pinch cayenne
2/3 cup fresh or thawed frozen corn kernels
1/4 cup chopped seeded red bell pepper
1/2 tablespoon minced seeded jalapeño pepper (wear gloves to prevent irritation)
1/4 cup grated Chihuahua or Monterey Jack cheese
1/4 cup reduced-fat sour cream
2 tablespoons chopped fresh cilantro

**1.** Preheat the oven to 450°F. Whisk together the egg substitute and masa harina in a bowl, then whisk in the buttermilk, butter, salt, and cayenne. Fold in the corn kernels, red bell pepper, jalapeño, and cheese. Spray 4 (1¼-cup) ramekins with nonstick spray and pour 2/3 cup of the batter into each. Put the ramekins on a baking sheet and bake until browned and puffed, about 20 minutes. Run a knife around the inside of the ramekins and unmold each cake onto a plate.

**2.** Mix together the sour cream and cilantro, then dollop on top of the cakes. Serve immediately.

Per serving (1 cake with about 1 tablespoon sour cream mixture): 167 Cal, 7 g Fat, 4 g Sat Fat, 23 mg Chol, 490 mg Sod, 15 g Carb, 1 g Fib, 12 g Prot, 163 mg Calc. **POINTS** value: **4.**

Masa harina is flour made from the dried corn-based dough used to make tortillas. Find masa harina in many supermarkets or in Hispanic groceries.

Santa Fe Corn-and-Cheddar Cakes

# Creamed Corn and Cheese Soufflé

**MAKES 4 SERVINGS**

The variations on this soufflé are endless. If you like, add some chopped Canadian bacon or chopped frozen spinach, thawed and squeezed dry. Serve this with a garden salad for a delicious and satisfying brunch.

2 cups low-fat (1%) milk
1 tablespoon butter
½ cup cornmeal
1 (14.75-ounce) can creamed corn
1 cup shredded reduced-fat cheddar cheese
4 egg yolks
4 egg whites, at room temperature
¼ teaspoon cream of tartar

**1.** Bring the milk and butter to a boil in a large nonstick saucepan over medium-high heat. Slowly add the cornmeal in a thin, steady stream, whisking constantly. Reduce the heat and continue stirring until the mixture is thickened and smooth, about 5 minutes. Remove the pan from the heat and stir in the corn and cheese. Add the egg yolks, one at a time, stirring until blended. Transfer the mixture to a bowl and let cool slightly.

**2.** Preheat the oven to 375°F. Spray a 2-quart baking dish with nonstick spray.

**3.** With an electric mixer on high speed, beat the egg whites until foamy; add the cream of tartar and beat until stiff but not grainy. Stir one-fourth of the egg whites into the cornmeal mixture. Fold in the remaining egg whites with a rubber spatula. Scrape the mixture into the baking dish. Bake until puffed and cooked through, about 35 minutes. Serve at once.

Per serving (¼ of soufflé): 380 Cal, 15 g Fat, 7 g Sat Fat, 241 mg Chol, 630 mg Sod, 40 g Carb, 3 g Fib, 22 g Prot, 388 mg Calc. **POINTS** value: **8.**

**COOK TO COOK** You'll get increased volume from the egg whites if you allow them to come to room temperature before beating. Make sure to use a large rubber spatula to thoroughly fold the egg whites into the corn mixture; cut down to the bottom of the bowl, lift, and turn the whites over, turning the bowl as you go.

# Lemony Cheese Blintzes

An 8-inch skillet will yield the perfect-size pancakes for these citrusy blintzes, finished with a quick, colorful raspberry sauce instead of the usual dollop of sour cream. For a nutty accent, add ½ teaspoon almond extract to the batter along with the milk.

2 tablespoons butter, melted

1 large egg

1 cup fat-free milk

¼ teaspoon salt

3 egg whites

⅓ cup all-purpose flour

¼ cup whole-wheat flour

2½ cups fat-free ricotta cheese

2½ tablespoons honey

½ tablespoon vanilla extract

½ tablespoon grated lemon zest

1 tablespoon + ¼ cup sugar

1 (10-ounce) package frozen raspberries in syrup, thawed

1 teaspoon fresh lemon juice

1. Combine the butter, egg, milk, salt, and 2 of the egg whites in a bowl. Whisk in the flours. Set aside for about 10 minutes to thicken.

2. For the filling, combine the third egg white, the ricotta, honey, vanilla, lemon zest, and 1 tablespoon of the sugar in another bowl. Mix well, cover, and refrigerate 30 minutes.

3. Heat a small nonstick skillet over medium heat. Swirl in 3 tablespoons of the batter. Cook until the edges are firm and the pancake is very lightly browned, about 1 minute. Slide the pancake out onto a plate. Repeat with the remaining batter, making a total of 12 pancakes. Meanwhile, put a heavy-gauge nonstick baking sheet into the oven and preheat the oven to 400°F.

4. Mound 3 tablespoons of the chilled filling in the center of a pancake. Fold the bottom up over the filling, fold the sides in, and roll up the pancake. Repeat the process to fill the remaining 11 blintzes. Spray the heated baking sheet with nonstick spray and place the blintzes on it. Bake the blintzes 5 minutes, spray them with nonstick spray, turn over, and cook until well browned, about 3 minutes longer.

5. To make the sauce, puree the raspberries with their juices, the remaining ¼ cup sugar, and the lemon juice in a food processor or blender. Pour into a small saucepan. Bring to a boil over medium-high heat and boil sauce for 1 minute. Drizzle over the blintzes.

Per serving (2 blintzes with about 3 tablespoons sauce): 288 Cal, 5 g Fat, 3 g Sat Fat, 47 mg Chol, 203 mg Sod, 40 g Carb, 1 g Fib, 21 g Prot, 167 mg Calc. *POINTS* value: *6.*

Skillet Apple and
Raisin Pancake

# Skillet Apple and Raisin Pancake

**MAKES 6 SERVINGS**

Tart green apples and sweet raisins pair beautifully in this harvest-style breakfast, perfect to serve on a chilly morning. Be creative and try different combinations of fruits, such as a delicious mix of apples and pears or peaches and plums.

1 tablespoon butter

4 Granny Smith apples, peeled, cored, and thinly sliced

¼ cup golden raisins

¼ cup apple juice

2 tablespoons granulated sugar

¼ teaspoon ground cinnamon

1 teaspoon vanilla extract

1 cup low-fat milk

2 large eggs

2 egg whites

¼ teaspoon salt

1 cup all-purpose flour

Confectioners' sugar for dusting

**1.** Preheat the oven to 425°F.

**2.** Melt the butter in a large ovenproof skillet over medium-high heat. Add the apples, raisins, apple juice, 1 tablespoon of the granulated sugar, and the cinnamon; cook, stirring frequently, until the apples are tender and the liquid has evaporated, about 10 minutes. Stir in the vanilla extract. Remove from the heat.

**3.** Beat together the milk, eggs, egg whites, salt, and the remaining 1 tablespoon granulated sugar in a medium bowl. Gradually whisk in the flour until blended and smooth. Pour the batter over the hot apple mixture. Bake 20 minutes. Reduce oven temperature to 350°F; bake until puffed and golden, about 15 minutes longer. Sprinkle with confectioners' sugar. Serve warm or at room temperature.

Per serving (⅙ pancake): 233 Cal, 5 g Fat, 2 g Sat Fat, 78 mg Chol, 171 mg Sod, 42 g Carb, 2 g Fib, 7 g Prot, 71 mg Calc. **POINTS** value: **5.**

COOK
TO
COOK

For an easy way to core apples, cut the apple in half and use a melon baller to scoop out the core and pits. This recipe is traditionally baked in a cast-iron skillet. If you don't have one, make sure the handle of your skillet is ovenproof, or cover with heavy-duty foil before putting the pan in the oven.

what's for breakfast?

# Orange-Berry Crêpes with Ricotta Cream

**MAKES 4 SERVINGS**

Reminiscent of crêpes suzette, this dish makes an elegant yet substantial brunch.
The berries add delicious flavor (not to mention a good dose of fiber, vitamins, and
minerals), and the orange-scented ricotta adds an appealing creamy contrast (as well
as a touch of protein and calcium).

1 cup fat-free milk

2 large eggs

1 cup all-purpose flour

2 teaspoons canola oil

¼ teaspoon salt

1 cup part-skim
ricotta cheese

2 tablespoons
confectioners' sugar

3 tablespoons fresh
orange juice

3 teaspoons grated
orange zest

2 cups fresh blueberries

1 cup fresh raspberries

2 tablespoon packed light
brown sugar

1 tablespoon orange liqueur
or vanilla extract

2 tablespoons toasted
sliced almonds

**1.** To make crêpes, beat the milk, eggs, flour, oil, and salt in
a medium bowl until smooth; let stand at least 15 minutes.
**2.** Spray a crêpe pan or 6-inch nonstick skillet with
nonstick spray; heat over medium-high heat until a drop
of water sizzles. Pour in 2 tablespoons of the batter and
swirl to cover the pan. Cook until the underside is set,
about 30 seconds. Flip and cook until lightly browned,
about 1 minute longer. Slide the crêpe onto wax paper.
Repeat with the remaining batter, making a total of
12 crêpes; stack the crêpes between sheets of wax paper to
prevent them from sticking to one another.
**3.** To make the ricotta cream, combine the ricotta cheese,
confectioners' sugar, 2 tablespoons of the orange juice, and
1 teaspoon of the orange zest in a small bowl.
**4.** Combine the blueberries, raspberries, brown sugar,
liqueur or extract, and the remaining 1 tablespoon orange
juice and 2 teaspoons orange zest in a large skillet; bring
to a boil. Reduce the heat and simmer, uncovered, until
slightly thickened, about 2 minutes. Fold the crêpes into
quarters and place in the sauce. Simmer until the crêpes
are hot, turning them once in the sauce, about 2 minutes.
Serve with the ricotta cream and sprinkle with almonds.

Per serving (3 crêpes with about ½ cup sauce and ¼ cup ricotta
cream): 408 Cal, 12 g Fat, 4 g Sat Fat, 126 mg Chol, 293 mg Sod,
58 g Carb, 5 g Fib, 17 g Prot, 286 mg Calc. **POINTS** value: **8.**

meals in minutes

★ ★ ★ ★ ★ ★ ★ ★ ★ ★ ★ ★ ★ ★ ★ ★ ★ ★ ★ ★ ★ ★ ★ ★ ★ ★ ★ ★ ★ ★ ★ ★ ★ ★ ★ ★ ★

# how to cook an egg

What's for breakfast? Aside from the delicious recipes in this chapter, you can't go wrong with a perfectly cooked egg or two. So we went right to the experts to bring you the real deal on proper egg cookery. Here, from the American Egg Board, the right way to scramble, fry, or poach them.

**SCRAMBLED EGGS** In a small bowl, beat together 2 eggs and 2 tablespoons fat-free or low-fat (1%) milk with salt and pepper to taste, until blended. In a 7–8-inch pan over medium heat, heat 1 teaspoon butter or cooking oil (or use nonstick spray) until a drop of water sizzles. Pour in egg mixture. As mixture begins to set, gently draw an inverted pancake turner completely across the bottom and sides of the pan, forming large, soft curds. Continue cooking until eggs are thickened and no visible liquid egg remains. Do not stir constantly.

**FRIED EGGS** In a 7–8-inch pan over medium-high heat, heat 1–2 teaspoons butter or cooking oil (or use nonstick spray) until a drop of water sizzles. Break and slip 2 eggs into pan. Immediately reduce heat to low. Cook slowly until whites are completely set and yolks begin to thicken but are not hard, covering tightly with a lid (adding 1 teaspoon water after edges turn white for steam-basted, if desired), spooning butter over the eggs to baste or turning the eggs to cook both sides. For over easy or over hard, gently lift eggs with a pancake turner and flip upside down into the pan to cook the second sides.

**POACHED EGGS** In a saucepan or skillet, bring 2–3 inches of water, fat-free or low-fat (1%) milk, reduced-fat broth, tomato juice, or other liquid to boiling. Reduce heat to keep water simmering. Break cold eggs, 1 at a time, into a custard cup or saucer or break several into a bowl. Holding dish close to water's surface, slip eggs into water. Cook until whites are completely set and yolks begin to thicken but are not hard, 3–5 minutes. With slotted spoon, lift out eggs. Drain in the spoon or on paper towels.

★ ★ ★ ★ ★ ★ ★ ★ ★ ★ ★ ★ ★ ★ ★ ★ ★ ★ ★ ★ ★ ★ ★ ★ ★ ★ ★ ★ ★ ★ ★ ★ ★ ★ ★ ★ ★

# just a bite

WHATEVER YOUR CRAVING, THESE EASY-TO-MAKE
NIBBLES FIT THE BILL—DELICIOUSLY

# Garlicky White Bean Dip

**MAKES 4 SERVINGS**

This simple yet luscious dip is ideal for everyday snacking, along with plenty of crunchy, no–*POINTS* value veggies like celery sticks, bell pepper strips, steamed broccoli or cauliflower florets, and Belgian endive leaves. It also makes a delicious sandwich spread for whole-wheat pita breads. The dip keeps in the refrigerator for up to three days.

1 (15$\frac{1}{2}$-ounce) can
   white beans, rinsed
   and drained
2 garlic cloves, chopped
1 tablespoon extra-virgin
   olive oil
$\frac{3}{4}$ teaspoon ground cumin
$\frac{1}{2}$ teaspoon salt
$\frac{1}{4}$ teaspoon freshly
   ground pepper

Process the beans, garlic, oil, cumin, salt, and pepper in a food processor until smooth. Transfer the mixture to a medium bowl and refrigerate, covered, until ready to serve.

Per serving ($\frac{1}{4}$ cup): 138 Cal, 4 g Fat, 1 g Sat Fat, 0 mg Chol, 472 mg Sod, 20 g Carb, 5 g Fib, 7 g Prot, 74 mg Calc. *POINTS* value: *2.*

meals in minutes

# Goat Cheese Crostini

**MAKES 4 SERVINGS**

Although these Tuscan-style toasts are delicious as they are, broiling until the cheese just begins to brown, 1 to 2 minutes, will enhance the flavor. If you don't broil the crostini, they can be made 15 to 20 minutes ahead.

¼ cup goat cheese
1 tablespoon chopped flat-leaf parsley
⅛ teaspoon freshly ground pepper
1 garlic clove, peeled
1 teaspoon olive oil
8 (½-inch-thick) baguette slices, toasted

In a small bowl, combine the goat cheese, parsley, and pepper. Press in the garlic with a garlic press, then add the oil and mix until smooth. Spread on the baguette slices.

Per serving (2 crostini): 200 Cal, 7 g Fat, 3 g Sat Fat, 11 mg Chol, 378 mg Sod, 27 g Carb, 2 g Fib, 8 g Prot, 83 mg Calc. *POINTS* value: *4.*

 Chervil, a member of the parsley family, has a mild anise flavor; if you like, substitute an equal amount for the parsley. For a flavor boost, use roasted garlic if you have some on hand.

just a bite

Tuna Crostini and
Marinated Shellfish
in Endive

# Tuna Crostini

**MAKES 8 SERVINGS**

Crostini, which means "little toasts" in Italian, are usually just brushed with olive oil. But to perk up the palate, we've added a topping with fresh tuna, olives, tomato, and anchovy. Use a dark Mediterranean olive (niçoise could be substituted for kalamata), but make sure to choose a variety packed in vinegar rather than oil to save on fat. Why not serve these along with Marinated Shellfish in Endive [see page 50]?

³/₄ **pound tuna steak**
**Juice of 1 lemon**
1 **teaspoon anchovy paste**
¹/₄ **teaspoon freshly ground pepper**
1 **plum tomato, chopped**
4 **scallions, thinly sliced**
6 **kalamata olives, pitted and chopped**
2 **tablespoons chopped flat-leaf parsley**
8 **(¹/₂-inch-thick) slices Italian bread, halved crosswise, lightly toasted**

**1.** Spray the broiler rack with nonstick spray; preheat the broiler. Broil the tuna 4 inches from the heat until just opaque in the center, about 5 minutes on each side.

**2.** In a large bowl, combine the lemon juice, anchovy paste, and pepper. Flake in the tuna, then add the tomato, scallions, olives, and parsley; toss to combine. Mound onto the bread slices.

Per serving (2 crostini): 103 Cal, 2 g Fat, 0 g Sat Fat, 1 mg Chol, 227 mg Sod, 18 g Carb, 2 g Fib, 4 g Prot, 47 mg Calc. *POINTS* value: *2.*

For a stronger anchovy taste, substitute three anchovy fillets, rinsed, patted dry, and minced, for the paste. If you find salt-packed anchovies (available at Greek or Italian markets), use them; they're far superior in flavor to the usual tinned variety.

# Portobello and Onion Toasts

**MAKES 4 SERVINGS**

These savory toasts are topped with fontina—a semisoft, creamy cow's-milk cheese that melts easily and has a mild, nutty taste. For best flavor, choose Italian fontina if you can get it. Alternatively, substitute shredded reduced-fat cheddar or mozzarella.

2 teaspoons olive oil
³/4 pound portobello
   mushrooms, stems
   removed, sliced
1 onion, thinly sliced
1 garlic clove, chopped
¼ teaspoon salt
¼ cup dry vermouth
4 (¹/2-inch-thick) slices
   Italian bread, toasted
¼ cup shredded
   fontina cheese

**1.** Heat the oil in a large nonstick skillet over medium-high heat. Add the mushrooms, onion, garlic, and salt and cook, stirring occasionally, until the mushrooms and onion are very tender, about 8 minutes. Stir in the vermouth and cook over medium heat, stirring occasionally, until the mushrooms and onions are golden brown and any liquid has evaporated, about 5 minutes.

**2.** Preheat the broiler.

**3.** Spoon the mushroom mixture onto the toasted bread. Sprinkle with the cheese. Broil the toasts 4 inches from the heat until the cheese is melted and bubbly, about 4 minutes. Serve at once.

Per serving (1 toast): 141 Cal, 5 g Fat, 2 g Sat Fat, 6 mg Chol, 310 mg Sod, 18 g Carb, 2 g Fib, 5 g Prot, 76 mg Calc. **POINTS** value: **3.**

meals in minutes

# Smoked Salmon Melba Toasts

**MAKES 1 SERVING**

Remember when melba toast screamed "diet food"? Not with *our* elegant twist. Substitute thinly sliced prosciutto for the smoked salmon if you prefer.

1 tablespoon light cream cheese or Neufchâtel

5 sesame melba toast rounds

2 tablespoons finely chopped seedless cucumber

1 tablespoon finely chopped red onion

½ ounce thinly sliced smoked salmon, cut into strips

Spread the cheese on the toast rounds. Top with the cucumber, onion, and salmon.

Per serving (5 toasts): 120 Cal, 4 g Fat, 2 g Sat Fat, 14 mg Chol, 265 mg Sod, 14 g Carb, 1 g Fib, 6 g Prot, 20 mg Calc. *POINTS* value: *3.*

**COOK TO COOK** Smoked salmon is salmon that has been cured through a smoking process in either hot or cool temperatures. Hot-smoking takes from 6 to 12 hours, cold-smoking from 1 day up to 3 weeks. So what's lox? It's salmon that has been cold-smoked and cured in brine (sometimes with added sugar).

# Avocado Boats with Salsa

**MAKES 8 SERVINGS**

This is a fiber-and-vitamin-filled treat for avocado lovers. Choose Haas avocados from California or Mexico, which have a smooth and creamy, full-flavored flesh. Avocados are rich in fiber, potassium, folic acid and other B-vitamins, and vitamin E. Their "good" fats are recommended as part of a heart-healthy diet.

1 **small tomato, diced**
2 **tablespoons minced red onion**
1 **tablespoon chopped fresh cilantro**
1 **tablespoon red-wine vinegar**
1/8 **teaspoon salt**
2 **ripe avocados, pitted, cut in quarters, lengthwise, then peeled**
4 **teaspoons fat-free sour cream**
**Cilantro sprigs (optional)**

Combine the tomato, onion, cilantro, vinegar, and salt in a small bowl. Spoon the tomato mixture onto the avocado quarters. Top each quarter with about 1/2 teaspoon of the sour cream and a cilantro sprig (if using). Serve at once.

Per serving (1 filled avocado quarter): 75 Cal, 6 g Fat, 1 g Sat Fat, 0 mg Chol, 43 mg Sod, 4 g Carb, 3 g Fib, 1 g Prot, 12 mg Calc. *POINTS* value: *1.*

*meals in minutes*

To remove the pit from an avocado, cut the avocado in half lengthwise and twist the halves apart. With the blade of a large chef's knife, make a quick downward stroke into the pit and twist. The pit should come out cleanly, attaching itself to the knife.

Avocado Boats
with Salsa

# Zesty Turkey Tostadas

**MAKES 6 SERVINGS**

For the best flavor, look for a smoked turkey breast that's still on the bone. (You'll find it in your supermarket's meat section, near the other turkey products.) We call for a fiery serrano chile in this recipe, but you can also use a jalapeño if it's more readily available.

½ **pound smoked turkey breast, chopped**
4 **plum tomatoes, diced**
¼ **cup chopped fresh cilantro**
4 **garlic cloves, peeled**
1 **small red onion, diced**
1 **serrano chile, seeded and minced (wear gloves to prevent irritation)**
**Juice of 1 lime**
2 **teaspoons chopped fresh oregano**
½ **teaspoon salt**
6 **soft corn tortillas**
3 **cups mesclun**

**1.** Preheat the oven to 400°F.

**2.** In a bowl, combine the turkey, tomatoes, and cilantro; press in the garlic with a garlic press. Stir in the onion, serrano chile, and lime juice, then the oregano and salt.

**3.** Place the tortillas directly onto the middle oven rack and bake until toasted, 5–6 minutes. Transfer to plates; top with the mesclun and the turkey mixture.

Per serving (1 tostada): 160 Cal, 3 g Fat, 1 g Sat Fat, 16 mg Chol, 759 mg Sod, 24 g Carb, 2 g Fib, 10 g Prot, 38 mg Calc. *POINTS* value: *3.*

If you have a toaster oven, the tortillas can be toasted in it for the same number of minutes as in a regular oven.

meals in minutes

# Hot-and-Spicy Chickpea Cakes

**MAKES 6 SERVINGS**

Sure they're great in soups and salads. But chickpeas' firm texture and mild, nutlike flavor also make a terrific bean cake, as this recipe deliciously demonstrates. Be sure to use high-quality fresh salsa, which you should be able to find in the dairy case of your supermarket. As a variation, you can also prepare the cakes with pinto beans.

1 (15-ounce) can chickpeas, rinsed and drained
⅓ cup reduced-fat sour cream
4 garlic cloves, peeled
1 teaspoon ground cumin
½ teaspoon salt
¾ teaspoon green hot sauce
¼ cup + 2 tablespoons white cornmeal
1½ cups prepared salsa

**1.** In a food processor, puree the chickpeas, sour cream, garlic, cumin, salt, hot sauce, and 2 tablespoons of the cornmeal; scrape into a bowl. Refrigerate, covered, until chilled, about 30 minutes.

**2.** Form the mixture into 6 (3-inch) round cakes, about ½-inch thick. Put the remaining ¼ cup cornmeal on a plate, and coat the cakes on both sides with the cornmeal.

**3.** Spray a large nonstick skillet with olive-oil nonstick spray and set over medium heat. Add the cakes and cook until browned on the bottom, 5–6 minutes. Spray the tops of the cakes, turn them over, and cook until brown on the other side, about 5 minutes longer. Spoon the salsa onto each of 6 plates, then top with a bean cake.

Per serving (1 cake with ¼ cup salsa): 137 Cal, 3 g Fat, 1 g Sat Fat, 4 mg Chol, 374 mg Sod, 23 g Carb, 4 g Fib, 6 g Prot, 76 mg Calc. ***POINTS*** value: **2.**

*just a bite*

 **COOK TO COOK** You can get the heat index you desire by choosing mild, medium, or hot salsa, as well as adjusting the hot-sauce amount to your taste.

# Tortilla Pinwheels

**MAKES 4 SERVINGS**

Like a chef's salad rolled up in a tortilla, these pinwheels are a tasty treat. If you like, substitute sliced turkey breast for the ham. You can also use any leafy greens you have on hand in place of the spinach.

1 cup torn fresh spinach
¹/₂ tomato, chopped
¹/₄ small onion, thinly sliced
1¹/₂ teaspoons cider vinegar
2 (6-inch) fat-free
   flour tortillas
2 ounces light cream
   cheese or Neufchâtel
2 tablespoons sliced
   pimiento-stuffed
   green olives
3 ounces sliced fat-free
   turkey ham

1. Combine the spinach, tomato, onion, and vinegar in a medium bowl.

2. Heat each tortilla in a dry skillet until softened and warm. Stack the tortillas between sheets of paper towels and cover with plastic wrap to prevent drying; set aside.

3. Spread the cream cheese onto the tortillas. Top with the olives, then the spinach mixture and ham. Roll the tortillas tightly and cut each one into 6 pieces, making a total of 12 pinwheels. Serve at once, or refrigerate, covered, until ready to serve.

Per serving (3 pinwheels): 109 Cal, 5 g Fat, 3 g Sat Fat, 23 mg Chol, 459 mg Sod, 8 g Carb, 1 g Fib, 7 g Prot, 46 mg Calc. *POINTS* value: *2.*

meals in minutes

# All-Veggie Nachos

**MAKES 6 SERVINGS**

When you're ready for a quiet night at home watching a favorite movie, here's a popular snack the whole family will appreciate. Substitute black beans for the pinto beans if you prefer. For a spicier version, add some minced jalapeños and use hot salsa instead of mild.

1 (15-ounce) can pinto beans, rinsed and drained

1 (8-ounce) can corn kernels, drained

2 tablespoons (from a 4-ounce can) chopped green chiles

1 tablespoon chili powder

1/2 teaspoon ground cumin

1/2 cup shredded reduced-fat sharp cheddar cheese

2 cups low-fat baked tortilla chips

2 cups shredded romaine lettuce

1 tomato, chopped

1/4 cup light sour cream

1/4 cup mild salsa

2 tablespoons chopped pitted ripe olives

2 tablespoons chopped fresh cilantro (optional)

1. Combine the beans, corn, chiles, chili powder, and cumin in a medium nonstick saucepan. Cook over medium heat, stirring frequently, until hot. Stir in the cheese until melted.

2. Arrange the tortilla chips on a large plate. Spoon the bean mixture over the chips, then top with the lettuce, tomato, sour cream, salsa, olives, and cilantro (if using). Serve at once.

Per serving (1/6 of nachos): 174 Cal, 4 g Fat, 2 g Sat Fat, 8 mg Chol, 394 mg Sod, 28 g Carb, 6 g Fib, 9 g Prot, 125 mg Calc. **POINTS** value: **3.**

just a bite

# Spinach-Stuffed Mushrooms

**MAKES 4 SERVINGS**

These festive iron-rich bites get their singular flavor punch from fresh oregano, nutmeg, and luscious melted cheese.

1 (10-ounce) bag triple-washed spinach, rinsed (do not dry)
1 large egg
2 tablespoons plain dried bread crumbs
1 tablespoon fat-free milk
1 teaspoon chopped fresh oregano
¼ teaspoon salt
⅛ teaspoon freshly ground pepper
⅛ teaspoon ground nutmeg
4 large white mushrooms, stems removed
¼ cup shredded Monterey Jack cheese

**1.** Preheat the oven to 400°F. Spray a baking dish with nonstick cooking spray.

**2.** Heat a large skillet over high heat. Add the spinach and cook, stirring as needed, until wilted, 2–3 minutes. Transfer to a cutting board and chop, then transfer to a bowl; mix in the egg, bread crumbs, milk, oregano, salt, pepper, and nutmeg.

**3.** Place the mushrooms, caps up, in the baking dish. Bake 5 minutes. Turn the mushrooms caps down; stuff with the spinach mixture, then sprinkle with the cheese. Bake until the cheese is melted and browned, about 15 minutes longer.

Per serving (1 mushroom): 81 Cal, 4 g Fat, 2 g Sat Fat, 53 mg Chol, 285 mg Sod, 7 g Carb, 1 g Fib, 6 g Prot, 148 mg Calc. ***POINTS*** value: *2.*

If you prefer, use large cremini mushrooms instead of the white variety, but don't use portobellos (they're too big). Monterey Jack cheese melts particularly well. If you like, use a flavored version, such as pepper-Jack.

# Crab Cakes on Greens

**MAKES 4 SERVINGS**

Here's a delicate and delicious way to start a fancy company dinner. Or double the recipe and form into smallish cakes for bite-size hors d'oeuvres your guests will love.

1 red bell pepper, seeded
   and coarsely chopped
4 scallions, coarsely
   chopped
1 celery stalk, coarsely
   chopped
2 large eggs
2 egg whites
2 tablespoons reduced-fat
   mayonnaise
1 tablespoon
   Worcestershire sauce
½ teaspoon crushed
   red pepper
6 ounces French bread,
   made into crumbs
   (3 cups)
½ pound cooked lump
   crabmeat, picked over
2 teaspoons canola oil
4 cups mesclun
4 lemon wedges

1. Pulse the bell pepper, scallions, celery, eggs, egg whites, mayonnaise, Worcestershire sauce, and crushed red pepper in a food processor until finely chopped. Transfer to a medium bowl.

2. Stir in the bread crumbs and crabmeat. Cover and refrigerate until the bread absorbs the liquid, at least 10 minutes or overnight.

3. Shape the mixture into 12 patties. Heat 1 teaspoon of the oil in a large nonstick skillet over medium-high heat. Add 6 patties and cook until golden and heated through, 3–4 minutes on each side. Repeat with the remaining oil and patties.

4. Serve the crab cakes on the mesclun, garnished with the lemon wedges.

Per serving (3 crab cakes with 1 cup mesclun): 291 Cal, 10 g Fat, 2 g Sat Fat, 165 mg Chol, 596 mg Sod, 28 g Carb, 4 g Fib, 22 g Prot, 167 mg Calc. *POINTS* value: *6.*

just a bite

# California Sushi Rolls

**MAKES 6 SERVINGS**

Sushi is surprisingly easy to make at home. Most of the ingredients, including sushi rice, rice vinegar, wasabi (green horseradish) powder, and nori (paper-thin sheets of dried seaweed), can be found in Asian groceries. Fat-free surimi, also called imitation crabmeat, is available in your supermarket's seafood section.

$2\frac{1}{4}$ cups water

2 cups sushi rice, rinsed

$\frac{1}{2}$ cup seasoned rice vinegar

1 tablespoon toasted sesame seeds

3 tablespoons warm water

2 tablespoons reduced-sodium soy sauce

2 teaspoons wasabi powder

1 teaspoon Asian (dark) sesame oil

1 teaspoon grated peeled fresh ginger

4 (7 x 8-inch) nori sheets

$\frac{1}{2}$ cucumber, peeled and cut into thin strips

$\frac{1}{2}$ avocado, peeled, pitted, and cut into thin strips

4 ounces surimi, cut into thin strips

Pickled ginger (optional)

1. Bring the water and rice to a boil in a medium saucepan. Reduce the heat and simmer, covered, until the rice is tender and the liquid is absorbed, about 20 minutes. Transfer the rice to a large bowl. Stir in the vinegar and sesame seeds. Let stand until cool enough to handle.

2. Meanwhile, to prepare the wasabi dipping sauce, whisk together the warm water, soy sauce, wasabi powder, sesame oil, and grated ginger until blended. Set aside.

3. Place a sheet of nori lengthwise, shiny-side down, onto rolling mat. Dampen hands with water and spread 1 cup of the rice mixture onto the nori, leaving a $\frac{1}{2}$-inch border across the top. Make a $\frac{1}{4}$-inch-deep indentation crosswise along the center of the rice; place one-quarter each of the cucumber, avocado, and surimi into the groove of the rice.

4. Hold the filling in place with your fingers as you curl the mat forward with your thumbs until the two ends of the nori overlap, forming a cylinder. Applying gentle but even pressure to the mat, remove the roll from the mat. Cut into 6 pieces with a very sharp knife, moistening knife with water between each cut. Repeat with the remaining nori, rice, cucumber, avocado, and surimi. Serve rolls with the dipping sauce and pickled ginger (if using).

Per serving (4 pieces with about $1\frac{1}{2}$ teaspoons dipping sauce): 314 Cal, 4 g Fat, 1 g Sat Fat, 6 mg Chol, 381 mg Sod, 59 g Carb, 3 g Fib, 9 g Prot, 38 mg Calc. **POINTS** value: **6.**

just a bite

# Parma Salad with Melon Dressing

**MAKES 6 SERVINGS**

This vibrant medley of vegetables and Parma ham, or prosciutto, is deliciously topped with a unique melon-based dressing—an intriguing twist on the typical Italianesque pairing of prosciutto di Parma and melon.

meals in minutes

12 asparagus spears
1 tablespoon water
8 cups mesclun
¼ pound prosciutto di Parma, shredded
1 red bell pepper, seeded and thinly sliced
1 cup chopped cantaloupe
2 tablespoons tarragon vinegar
2 teaspoons olive oil
¼ teaspoon salt
¼ teaspoon sugar
⅛ teaspoon crushed red pepper

1. Snap off the bottoms of the asparagus spears. Combine the spears and water in a covered microwavable dish and microwave on High 1 minute. Cut the asparagus into chunks on the diagonal.

2. In a large salad bowl, combine the asparagus, mesclun, ham, and bell pepper. Puree the cantaloupe, vinegar, oil, salt, sugar, and crushed red pepper in a food processor or blender. Pour the dressing over the salad and toss to coat.

Per serving (about 1 cup): 97 Cal, 5 g Fat, 2 g Sat Fat, 11 mg Chol, 362 mg Sod, 8 g Carb, 3 g Fib, 6 g Prot, 54 mg Calc. **POINTS** value: **2.**

 If you don't have a microwave oven, lightly cook the asparagus in a steamer basket over boiling water for 5 minutes.

# Radicchio Bundles

**MAKES 4 SERVINGS**

When a dish has so few ingredients, you want to make sure those you use are of the highest quality. Seek out an Italian-style delicatessen to get authentic prosciutto di Parma and the freshest mozzarella.

12 radicchio leaves,
 blanched
2 ounces prosciutto di
 Parma, thinly sliced
 and halved
¼ pound fresh mozzarella
 cheese, thinly sliced

1. Preheat the oven to 350°F.

2. In the center of each radicchio leaf, place a piece of prosciutto and a slice of cheese. Fold the stem end of the leaf over the filling, then fold in the sides and roll up; secure each bundle with a toothpick. Place the bundles in a baking dish. Bake until the cheese is melted and the radicchio has given off its liquid, 20–25 minutes.

Per serving (3 bundles): 96 Cal, 5 g Fat, 3 g Sat Fat, 23 mg Chol, 340 mg Sod, 2 g Carb, 0 g Fib, 10 g Prot, 189 mg Calc. **POINTS** value: **2.**

just a bite

COOK TO COOK

Blanching radicchio makes it easier to work with. To blanch, bring a small saucepan of water to a boil. Core the radicchio as you would a tomato and place it in the boiling water for 10 seconds. Run briefly under cold water, then peel leaves from the core end.

# Marinated Shellfish in Endive

**MAKES 6 SERVINGS**

This zesty starter is similar to seviche, except the seafood is lightly cooked for safety. Feel free to vary the seafood with whatever looks best at your fish market. Try such alternatives or additions as calamari rings (not tentacles) or chunks of red snapper or sole.

½ red bell pepper, seeded and diced

2 scallions, thinly sliced

1 tablespoon chopped fresh cilantro

⅛ teaspoon crushed red pepper

½ cup dry white wine

1 bay leaf

¾ cup water

¼ pound shrimp, peeled, deveined, and diced

¼ pound bay scallops

¼ teaspoon salt

Juice of 2 limes

6 large Belgian endive leaves

1. In a bowl, combine the bell pepper, scallions, cilantro, and crushed red pepper.

2. In a medium saucepan, combine the wine, bay leaf, and water; bring to a boil and boil 3 minutes. Reduce the heat and add the shrimp and scallops; simmer until the shrimp and scallops are opaque in the center, about 1 minute. Drain, discarding the bay leaf; add the seafood to the vegetables. Stir in the salt, then mix in the lime juice. Spoon into the endive leaves.

Per serving (1 endive leaf with about ⅓ cup shellfish mixture): 78 Cal, 1 g Fat, 0 g Sat Fat, 35 mg Chol, 169 mg Sod, 7 g Carb, 3 g Fib, 8 g Prot, 53 mg Calc. **POINTS** value: *1.*

*meals in minutes*

# Shrimp in Lime-Butter Sauce

**MAKES 4 SERVINGS**

Using scissors or a small paring knife to cut the shells will facilitate the cleaning and peeling of the shrimp for this simple, tasty dish. Like most seafood, shrimp are done when they turn opaque in the center.

1 **pound large shrimp**
4 **garlic cloves, minced**
1 **cup chicken broth**
2 **tablespoons fresh lime juice**
1 **tablespoon butter, cut up**
¼ **cup chopped fresh cilantro**
⅛ **teaspoon salt**
¼ **teaspoon coarsely ground black pepper**

1. To peel the shrimp, make a cut along the outer curved side of each; remove the shell, leaving the tail intact. Hold the shrimp under cold running water to rinse out the black veins. Pat them dry with paper towels.

2. Spray a nonstick skillet with olive-oil nonstick spray and heat over medium heat, then add the shrimp. Cook until the shrimp are just opaque in the center, 3–4 minutes on each side. Transfer the shrimp to a plate. Add the garlic and broth to the skillet and cook until the broth is reduced by one-half, 3–4 minutes. Stir in the lime juice and cook for 30 seconds. Add the shrimp and butter, stirring to blend. Add the cilantro and cook about 30 seconds longer to heat the shrimp through. Season with the salt and pepper. Drizzle the sauce over the shrimp.

Per serving (about 4 shrimp): 163 Cal, 6 g Fat, 2 g Sat Fat, 181 mg Chol, 492 mg Sod, 3 g Carb, 0 g Fib, 24 g Prot, 68 mg Calc. **POINTS** value: **4.**

just a bite

# Wild Mushroom Strudel

**MAKES 8 SERVINGS**

Cremini mushrooms are sometimes referred to as baby portobellos or simply
brown mushrooms. If you can't find them, substitute an equal weight of portobello
mushrooms, cut into chunks.

½ pound white mushrooms, stems removed

6 ounces cremini mushrooms, stems removed

3½ ounces shiitake mushrooms, stems removed

1 red onion, chunked

1 teaspoon dried thyme leaves

½ teaspoon dried coriander

½ teaspoon salt

½ teaspoon freshly ground pepper

1½ cup evaporated fat-free milk

½ cup dry white wine

4 (12 x 17-inch) sheets phyllo dough, at room temperature

**1.** In a food processor, finely chop the mushrooms and onion. Heat a medium nonstick skillet over medium-high heat. Add the mushrooms and onion and cook, stirring frequently, until the onion is softened, about 5 minutes. Stir in the thyme, coriander, salt, and pepper, then add the evaporated milk and wine. Simmer until the liquid is absorbed, 12–15 minutes. Transfer to a bowl; refrigerate, covered, until thickened and chilled, at least 1 hour.

**2.** Preheat oven to 375°F. Fit a baking sheet with a piece of parchment or wax paper. Put 1 sheet of the phyllo in the center and spray with nonstick spray. Layer the other 3 sheets on top, spraying between each. Spoon the mushroom filling onto a short end, leaving a ¼-inch border. Lift the short edge alongside the filling over the mixture and roll up into a log. Turn the log one-quarter turn so that it lies lengthwise in the center of the baking sheet; lightly spray the top. Bake until golden brown, 25–30 minutes. Cut into 8 (1½-inch) slices.

Per serving (1 slice): 67 Cal, 1 g Fat, 0 g Sat Fat, 1 mg Chol, 212 mg Sod, 11 g Carb, 1 g Fib, 3 g Prot, 10 mg Calc. **POINTS** value: **1.**

This elegant dish holds up well on a buffet. Bake the strudel 2 hours before serving so the flavors have time to blend.

meals in minutes

# Spicy Veal Skewers

**MAKES 6 SERVINGS**

These skewers, seasoned with paprika and pepper, are savory enough that they don't need a dipping sauce. So we suggest a high-quality Hungarian paprika for the richest flavor. Be warned that hot paprika is hot. When you see a recipe calling for this much, be sure to use sweet paprika (it's often not labeled as such, but simply "paprika").

1 cup dry red wine
2 scallions, cut into 1-inch lengths
2 tablespoons paprika
1 teaspoon freshly ground pepper
¼ teaspoon salt
8 sprigs parsley
4 garlic cloves, peeled
1 pound veal top round, trimmed of all visible fat and cut into 18 (1-inch) cubes

**1.** Soak 6 (8-inch) bamboo skewers in water for at least 1 hour. Meanwhile, combine the wine, scallions, paprika, pepper, salt, and parsley in a zip-close plastic bag; press in the garlic with a garlic press, then add the veal. Squeeze out the air and seal the bag; turn to coat the veal. Refrigerate, turning bag occasionally, at least 1 hour.

**2.** Spray the broiler rack with nonstick spray; preheat the broiler. Thread 3 cubes of veal onto each skewer, leaving about ½ inch between cubes. Broil the skewers 4 inches from the heat until well browned, 4–5 minutes. Turn the skewers and broil until browned on the second side, about 4 minutes longer.

Per serving (1 skewer): 132 Cal, 3 g Fat, 1 g Sat Fat, 60 mg Chol, 172 mg Sod, 4 g Carb, 1 g Fib, 16 g Prot, 39 mg Calc. **POINTS** value: **3.**

Cubed veal stew meat is from the same lean cut as top round. Don't hesitate to buy it if you're pressed for time.

# Papaya-Kiwi Smoothie

**MAKES 2 SERVINGS**

Well in this case, it's "just a sip." Here's a refreshing smoothie with a cool bonus:
It keeps well in the refrigerator for up to three days. Serve with fresh mint.

1 papaya, halved and
  seeds removed
2 kiwi fruits, halved
1 cup orange juice
4 teaspoons honey
2 teaspoons fresh lime
  or lemon juice
8 ice cubes

Scoop the papaya flesh and the kiwi fruit flesh into a
blender. Add the orange juice, honey, and lime juice; pulse
until smooth. Add the ice cubes and pulse the mixture
until slightly crushed.

Per serving (1½ cups): 205 Cal, 1 g Fat, 0 g Sat Fat, 0 mg Chol,
12 mg Sod, 52 g Carb, 6 g Fib, 3 g Prot, 70 mg Calc. **POINTS** value: **3.**

just a bite

# Maple Granola Bars

**MAKES 10 SERVINGS**

If you're looking for a pick-me-up between light meals, these portable bars are a great choice to have on hand. They're also an excellent addition to school lunches. Store them in an airtight container for up to a week.

3 cups quick-cooking rolled oats
1 cup raisins, chopped
1/2 cup sliced almonds, chopped
1 teaspoon ground cinnamon
1/2 teaspoon salt
1/4 cup maple syrup
1/4 cup honey
1/4 cup water
1 tablespoon packed dark brown sugar

1. Preheat the oven to 325°F. Spray a baking sheet with nonstick spray.

2. Combine the oats, raisins, almonds, cinnamon, and salt in a large bowl.

3. Bring the syrup, honey, water, and brown sugar to a boil in a small saucepan; remove from the heat. Pour over the oat mixture, stirring well to coat. With wet hands, shape the mixture into 10 (4-inch) logs. Place the logs on the baking sheet and flatten to 1/2-inch thickness.

4. Bake until the bars are slightly firm to the touch, about 30 minutes. Cool on the baking sheet 5 minutes; remove from the baking sheet and cool completely on a rack.

Per serving (1 bar): 220 Cal, 4 g Fat, 1 g Sat Fat, 0 mg Chol, 122 mg Sod, 43 g Carb, 4 g Fib, 5 g Prot, 45 mg Calc. **POINTS** value: **4.**

★ ★ ★ ★ ★ ★ ★ ★ ★ ★ ★ ★ ★ ★ ★ ★ ★ ★ ★ ★ ★ ★ ★ ★ ★ ★ ★ ★ ★ ★ ★

# super-fast meal makers

maybe you've no time to prepare a main course—or maybe you're just in the mood for a light meal. If so, one or more of these lickety-split, no-cook appetizers will fill the bill perfectly. Looking for quick and casual family fare? Make them all and serve buffet-style. Even the kids will love *these*.

**CUCUMBER DIP** (8 servings): Peel a large cucumber, slice lengthwise, and use a small spoon to scrape out and discard the seeds. Shred through the large holes of a box grater; place in a colander, sprinkle with 1/2 teaspoon salt, and press to squeeze out as much water as possible. Place in a bowl with 1 cup plain yogurt, 1/2 cup reduced-fat sour cream, and 1 teaspoon dried dill; stir to combine. Serve with raw vegetables and breadsticks. Per serving (1/4 cup dip with assorted veggies and 2 short breadsticks) *POINTS* value: *2.*

**SALAD-BAR ROLL-UPS** (8 servings): Spread 4 large flour tortillas each with 2 tablespoons fat-free cream cheese. Sprinkle each with 1/2 cup shredded carrots and 2 tablespoons each chopped black olives and pickled jalapeño peppers (from your supermarket salad bar). Roll up and slice 1-inch thick (you'll get about 8 slices per roll). Per serving (4 slices) *POINTS* value: *2.*

**TOMATO-HUMMUS BITES** (6 servings): Slice a pint of cherry tomatoes in half; trim a thin slice off the bottom of each half so it can stand cut-side up. Squeeze out the pulp from each half and discard. Spoon about 1/2 teaspoon prepared hummus into each half. Per serving (4 bites) *POINTS* value: *1/2.*

**STUFFED SMOKED-SALMON ROLLS** (4 servings): Line up on wax paper 1/4 pound of salmon slices to make 8 (4–6-inch-long) pieces. Then blend 1/2 cup fat-free cream cheese with 1/4 cup finely chopped chives. Place 1 tablespoon of mixture on one end of each salmon slice, gently roll up, and sprinkle with freshly ground pepper. Per serving (2 rolls) *POINTS* value: *2.*

just a bite

★ ★ ★ ★ ★ ★ ★ ★ ★ ★ ★ ★ ★ ★ ★ ★ ★ ★ ★ ★ ★ ★ ★ ★ ★ ★ ★ ★ ★ ★ ★

# ready, set, five!

MAIN MEALS, NEEDING VERY LITTLE PREP
TIME, ALL A THRIFTY *POINTS* VALUE OF 5 OR LESS

★ ★ ★ ★ ★ ★ ★ ★ ★ ★ ★ ★ ★ ★ ★ ★ ★ ★ ★ ★ ★ ★ ★ ★ ★ ★ ★ ★ ★ ★ ★ ★ ★ ★ ★

★ ★ ★ ★ ★ ★ ★ ★ ★ ★ ★ ★ ★ ★ ★ ★ ★ ★ ★ ★ ★ ★ ★ ★ ★ ★ ★ ★ ★ ★ ★ ★ ★ ★ ★

# Insalata Frutti di Mare

**MAKES 4 SERVINGS**

This versatile seafood salad can be prepared with whatever looks freshest from your fishmonger. Replace the squid with fresh bay scallops, cooked for the same length of time, if you prefer. Or substitute fresh cod, red snapper, or sea bass for the halibut.

1 cup water

1 cup dry white wine

3 (quarter-size) slices peeled fresh ginger

1/2 pound halibut fillets

1/4 pound medium shrimp, peeled and deveined

1/4 pound cleaned squid bodies, cut into 1/4-inch rings

1 large celery stalk, chopped

1/2 cup chopped seeded red bell pepper

2 tablespoons large capers, drained

2 tablespoons chopped fresh parsley

1 teaspoon finely chopped seeded jalapeño pepper (wear gloves to prevent irritation)

3 tablespoons fresh lemon juice

1/2 teaspoon grated lemon zest

4 teaspoons olive oil

1/4 teaspoon salt

1/8 teaspoon ground cumin

Pinch crushed red pepper

**1.** Bring the water, wine, and ginger to a boil in a medium saucepan. Boil 1 minute, then reduce the heat to medium. Add the halibut and cook 3 minutes. Add the shrimp and cook 1 minute, then add the squid and cook 1 minute longer. Discard the ginger. Strain and rinse the seafood briefly under cold water to stop the cooking. Break the halibut into pieces, then combine with the shrimp, squid, celery, bell pepper, capers, parsley, and jalapeño in a bowl.

**2.** To make the dressing, whisk together the lemon juice, lemon zest, oil, salt, cumin, and crushed red pepper. Pour the dressing over the salad and toss to coat. Cover and refrigerate 1 hour to chill before serving.

Per serving ($^3/_4$ cup): 212 Cal, 7 g Fat, 1 g Sat Fat, 127 mg Chol, 383 mg Sod, 5 g Carb, 1 g Fib, 23 g Prot, 68 mg Calc. **POINTS** value: **5.**

*meals in minutes*

# Pizza Provençal

**MAKES 8 SERVINGS**

Semolina is coarsely ground durum wheat (the type of wheat used to make pasta). It's even higher in protein than bread flour, so it will result in a very dense, chewy crust. If you have a choice, opt for Italian fontina cheese for the topping—the French and Danish versions aren't nearly as full-flavored.

  2 cups all-purpose flour
1⅓ cups semolina
  1 tablespoon kosher salt or
    ½ tablespoon table salt
  1 envelope quick-rise yeast
  ½ teaspoon sugar
1¼ cups hot tap water
  4 plum tomatoes, cut
    into rounds
  1 red onion, thinly sliced
 12 kalamata olives, pitted
    and chopped
  ¼ cup chopped fresh basil
  4 ounces fontina cheese,
    shredded (about ⅔ cup)

1. Combine the flour, semolina, salt, yeast, and sugar in a food processor. With machine running, drizzle water through the feed tube until the dough just forms a ball.
2. Spray a large bowl with nonstick spray; put the dough in the bowl. Cover lightly with plastic wrap and let the dough rise in a warm spot until it doubles in size and no longer springs back to the touch, about 20 minutes.
3. Meanwhile, preheat the oven to 450°F.
4. Cut the dough in half and place each piece on a 15-inch pizza pan. Press the dough with your fingertips to cover the pans completely. Layer the crusts with the tomatoes, onion, and olives; scatter with the basil and cheese. Bake until the crusts are golden and the cheese is melted and browned, 15–18 minutes.

Per serving (¼ of 1 pizza): 278 Cal, 5 g Fat, 2 g Sat Fat, 10 mg Chol, 200 mg Sod, 48 g Carb, 3 g Fib, 10 g Prot, 70 mg Calc. *POINTS* value: *5.*

Quick-rise yeast cuts the time needed for this dough to rise by a third. If you're planning to buy a pizza pan, choose one with holes, which allow the oven heat to crisp the bottom of the crust.

# Chili Blanco

**MAKES 6 SERVINGS**

Poblano chiles, cumin, and coriander stand in for the typical chili powder and provide the heat in this chicken and white-bean chili. If desired, dollop each serving with one tablespoon sour cream (and increase your *POINTS* value by 1).

2 poblano chiles
$^1/_2$ tablespoon olive oil
1 large yellow onion, chopped
4 large garlic cloves, minced
$^3/_4$ pound chicken breast, cut into chunks
$^1/_2$ pound white mushrooms, quartered
1 tablespoon ground cumin
2 teaspoons ground coriander
$^1/_2$ teaspoon salt
1 (15-ounce) can small white beans, rinsed and drained
1 (15-ounce) can Great Northern beans, rinsed and drained
1$^3/_4$ cups chicken broth
$^1/_4$ cup chopped fresh cilantro
$^1/_2$ tablespoon fresh lime juice

**1.** Preheat the broiler. Line a baking sheet with foil; place the chiles on the baking sheet. Broil 5 inches from the heat, turning occasionally with tongs, until lightly charred, about 10 minutes. Transfer the chiles to a bowl, cover, and let stand 5 minutes. Peel, seed, and chop the chiles. Set aside.

**2.** Heat the oil in a nonstick Dutch oven over medium-high heat. Add the onion and garlic and cook, stirring, until the onion is softened. Add the chicken, mushrooms, cumin, coriander, and salt; cook until the chicken is no longer pink and the mushrooms begin to soften, about 4 minutes. Add the beans, broth, and chiles. Cover and cook until flavors are blended, about 8 minutes. Uncover, reduce the heat, and cook until thickened, about 7 minutes longer. Stir in the cilantro and lime juice.

Per serving (about 1 cup): 196 Cal, 4 g Fat, 1 g Sat Fat, 34 mg Chol, 845 mg Sod, 26 g Carb, 8 g Fib, 22 g Prot, 87 mg Calc. *POINTS* value: *3.*

Vary the recipe (and in some cases its color) by using 3 to 3$^1/_2$ cups of any combination of cooked beans, such as pinto, navy, or red kidney, in place of the small white beans and Great Northern beans.

ready, set, five!

Mexican Chicken Salad and
Quick Jalapeño Corn Soup

# Mexican Chicken Salad

**MAKES 4 SERVINGS**

Toasted tortilla strips are a perfect garnish for this zesty salad. To make, spray both sides of a 10-inch flour tortilla with nonstick spray, cut it into small, thin strips (about 3 x 1$^1$/$_2$ inch), and scatter in a single layer on a baking sheet. Bake in a 400°F oven until golden, 6–7 minutes. Sprinkle the cooled strips over the salads (increase your *POINTS* value by 1), and serve with our Quick Jalapeño Corn Soup on page 89.

1 tablespoon fresh
   lime juice

4 teaspoons olive oil

2 garlic cloves, peeled

$^3$/$_4$ teaspoon chili powder

$^3$/$_4$ pound skinless boneless
   chicken breasts, poached
   and cut into 1-inch
   chunks

1 tomato, seeded and cut
   into $^1$/$_2$-inch cubes

1 avocado, peeled, pitted,
   and sliced

2 scallions, minced
   (white and light-green
   parts only)

2 tablespoons minced
   fresh cilantro

2 cups shredded
   romaine lettuce

**1.** To make the dressing, put the lime juice in a small bowl. Drizzle in the oil, whisking constantly. Press in the garlic with a garlic press and add the chili powder; whisk thoroughly.

**2.** In a large bowl combine the chicken, tomato, avocado, scallions, and cilantro. Pour the dressing over and toss to coat. Refrigerate, covered, until the flavors are blended, at least 2 hours.

**3.** Divide the lettuce among 4 plates and mound the chicken salad on top.

Per serving ($^1$/$_2$ cup lettuce and about $^3$/$_4$ cup chicken salad):
243 Cal, 14 g Fat, 2 g Sat Fat, 49 mg Chol, 77 mg Sod, 9 g Carb,
5 g Fib, 22 g Prot, 60 mg Calc. *POINTS* value: **5.**

**COOK TO COOK**

To poach the chicken, bring 1 cup chicken broth to a simmer in a medium saucepan over medium heat. Add the chicken breasts, cover, and simmer until cooked through, about 5 minutes on each side.

# Curried Chicken and Wild Rice Soup

**MAKES 6 SERVINGS**

Nutty-tasting, slightly chewy wild rice adds delicious dimension to this flavorful soup. Be sure to use light coconut milk, which has only a fraction of the fat of regular coconut milk; if you can't find it, use an equal amount of fat-free evaporated milk to which ½ teaspoon coconut extract has been added.

1⅓ cups water
⅓ cup wild rice
½ tablespoon olive oil
¾ pound chicken breast, cut into chunks
1 large yellow onion, cut into ½-inch chunks
2 celery stalks, cut on the diagonal into ¼-inch slices
12 baby carrots, quartered on the diagonal
2 large garlic cloves, minced
3½ cups chicken broth
1 tablespoon curry powder
⅛ teaspoon ground white pepper (optional)
½ cup chopped seeded red bell pepper
¼ cup light coconut milk
½ tablespoon rice vinegar
1 tablespoon chopped fresh cilantro

**1.** Bring the water to a boil in a small saucepan. Add the rice. Cover, reduce the heat, and simmer until just tender and a few grains have popped, 45–60 minutes.

**2.** Meanwhile, heat the oil in a nonstick Dutch oven over medium-high heat. Add the chicken and cook, stirring, until lightly browned. Add the onion, celery, carrots, and garlic. Cook until the onion is softened, about 3 minutes. Stir in the broth, curry powder, and white pepper (if using). Bring to a boil. Cover, reduce the heat, and simmer until the flavors blend, about 15 minutes. Stir in the wild rice, bell pepper, coconut milk, and vinegar. Serve, sprinkled with the cilantro.

Per serving (scant 1 cup): 156 Cal, 5 g Fat, 1 g Sat Fat, 36 mg Chol, 649 mg Sod, 13 g Carb, 2 g Fib, 16 g Prot, 36 mg Calc. **POINTS** value: **3.**

 Don't let too many grains of wild rice pop open—it's a sign the rice has been cooked too long. Since it will be added to the soup, it will continue to absorb liquid, so it's fine to undercook it slightly.

# Piedmontese Braised Turkey

**MAKES 6 SERVINGS**

The Piedmont region is in the northwestern part of Italy, bordering France and Switzerland. This preparation is typical of the red-wine braising done in this area. Serve the turkey with sautéed broccoli rabe and quick-cooking polenta for a hearty meal.

2 cups low-sodium
   chicken broth
1 cup dry red wine
1½ pounds turkey breast
   tenderloin
1 small red onion,
   thinly sliced
2 tablespoons chopped
   fresh sage
½ teaspoon salt
¼ teaspoon freshly
   ground pepper

**1.** In a medium nonstick skillet, bring the broth and wine to a boil and boil 2 minutes. Add the turkey, onion, and sage. Reduce the heat and simmer, covered, until the turkey is cooked through, about 15 minutes. Remove from the heat.

**2.** To make the gravy, transfer ¼ cup of the braising liquid to a small bowl and mix with the cornstarch. Transfer 1 cup of the braising liquid to a small saucepan; bring to a boil. Remove from heat and whisk in the dissolved cornstarch. Return to heat and cook until thickened and translucent, about 2 minutes. Stir in the salt and pepper.

**3.** Thinly slice the turkey and fan onto dinner plates. Scatter each plate with the onion, drizzle with the gravy, and serve at once.

Per serving (4 [1-ounce] slices turkey with about 3 tablespoons gravy):
177 Cal, 2 g Fat, 1 g Sat Fat, 72 mg Chol, 289 mg Sod, 4 g Carb,
1 g Fib, 29 g Prot, 36 mg Calc. *POINTS* value: *4.*

ready, set, five!

# Turkey Oaxaca

**MAKES 6 SERVINGS**

Mexican mole is an intense, dark sauce usually served with poultry. There are many variations of this spicy specialty, depending on its place of origin. Oaxaca is a town famous for its seven moles, including a chocolate or cocoa-infused rendition such as this one, which adds richness rather than sweetness.

4 dried ancho chiles

2 cups boiling water

1 medium white onion, cut into chunks

3 large garlic cloves, peeled

1 tablespoon unsweetened cocoa powder

1 teaspoon dried oregano

½ teaspoon dried thyme

½ teaspoon coarsely ground black pepper

¼ teaspoon anise seeds

1 (1³/₄–2-pound) boneless turkey breast

1 bay leaf

1 cinnamon stick (optional)

1 tablespoon masa harina

½ tablespoon fresh lime juice

**1.** Combine the ancho chiles and boiling water in a bowl, cover, and let steep until chiles are soft, about 30 minutes.

**2.** Meanwhile, preheat the oven to 350°F.

**3.** To make the mole, strain the ancho chiles, reserving the soaking liquid; then stem, core, seed, and devein them. Put the chiles and their soaking liquid into a food processor. Add the onion, garlic, cocoa, oregano, thyme, pepper, and anise seeds. Process to a puree, about 30 seconds.

**4.** Put the turkey breast into a heavy medium skillet with an ovenproof handle. Pour the mole over the breast and add the bay leaf and cinnamon stick (if using). Cover and bake until the turkey reaches an internal temperature of 170°F, about 1¼ hours.

**5.** Transfer the turkey to a cutting board. Discard the bay leaf and cinnamon stick. Transfer ¼ cup of the mole to a bowl and mix in the masa harina, then stir the mixture back into the pan. Stirring frequently, cook over medium heat until thickened, about 3 minutes. Stir in the lime juice. Slice the turkey breast and remove the skin. Divide the turkey slices among 6 dinner plates, and spoon the mole over the slices.

Per serving (4–5 [1-ounce] slices turkey with ¼ cup mole): 156 Cal, 2 g Fat, 0 g Sat Fat, 59 mg Chol, 52 mg Sod, 10 g Carb, 4 g Fib, 25 g Prot, 38 mg Calc. *POINTS* value: *2.*

meals in minutes

# Wheat Berries with Smoked Turkey and Fruit

**MAKES 4 SERVINGS**

Wheat berries are whole, unprocessed wheat kernels that add wonderful crunch and flavor to any salad. You can find them in natural-foods stores and specialty markets. High in protein, they will keep for up to a year in an airtight container stored in a cool, dark, and dry space.

2¼ cups water

1 cup wheat berries, rinsed

½ pound smoked turkey in one piece, cubed

2 nectarines, pitted and cubed

1 Granny Smith apple, cored and cubed

½ red onion, chopped

¼ cup orange juice

3 tablespoons cider vinegar

1 tablespoon Dijon mustard

1 tablespoon honey

½ (10-ounce) bag baby spinach, coarsely chopped

**1.** Bring the water to a boil in a medium saucepan. Stir in the wheat berries; reduce the heat and simmer, covered, until the berries are tender and the water is absorbed, 1½–2 hours. Fluff the wheat berries with a fork, then let stand 5 minutes.

**2.** Combine the wheat berries with the smoked turkey, nectarines, apple, and onion in a large bowl. Whisk together the orange juice, vinegar, mustard, and honey in a small bowl. Stir the juice mixture into the wheat berry mixture until blended.

**3.** Arrange the spinach on a platter. Spoon the wheat berries–turkey mixture on top. Serve at once.

Per serving (2 cups): 285 Cal, 3 g Fat, 1 g Sat Fat, 23 mg Chol, 765 mg Sod, 54 g Carb, 9 g Fib, 16 g Prot, 66 mg Calc. **POINTS** value: **5.**

*ready, set, five!*

If you're pressed for time, substitute bulgur wheat (it cooks in about 25 minutes), for the wheat berries.

# Orzo Pesto Salad

**MAKES 8 SERVINGS**

This low–*POINTS* value pesto is made with the orzo cooking liquid in place of oil; the hot water blanches the basil and arugula a bit, helping to retain their bright green color. Including arugula as well as basil adds a peppery accent and allows for the substitution of more assertively flavored walnuts in place of the typical pine nuts.

|  |
|---|
| 4 cups water |
| 1 1/2 cups orzo |
| 3/4 cup basil leaves |
| 2/3 cup arugula leaves |
| 2 garlic cloves, peeled |
| 1 tablespoon walnut pieces |
| 1 1/2 teaspoons salt |
| 1 cup dry white wine |
| 2 bay leaves |
| 3/4 pound turkey breast cutlets |
| 6 kalamata olives, pitted and slivered |
| 1 head radicchio, quartered, cored, and sliced |
| 16 cherry tomatoes, quartered |
| 3 tablespoons grated Parmesan cheese |
| 1/4 teaspoon coarsely ground black pepper |

**1.** Bring the water to a boil in a medium saucepan. Add the orzo, reduce the heat, and cook until al dente, about 5 minutes. Drain, reserving 1/2 cup of the cooking liquid, and put the orzo in a large bowl.

**2.** To make the pesto, combine the basil, arugula, garlic, walnuts, and 1 teaspoon of the salt in a food processor or blender. Add the reserved cooking liquid and puree. Stir 2 tablespoons of the pesto into the orzo.

**3.** Bring the wine and bay leaves to a boil in a medium skillet. Boil 1 minute, then reduce the heat to medium and add the turkey. Cover and poach until the turkey is cooked through, about 5 minutes. Drain, discarding the bay leaves. Chop the turkey and add it to the orzo. Stir in the olives and radicchio. Fold in the remaining pesto and then the cherry tomatoes. Add the Parmesan, pepper, and the remaining 1/2 teaspoon of salt; toss to combine.

Per serving (about 1 cup): 242 Cal, 6 g Fat, 1 g Sat Fat, 29 mg Chol, 559 mg Sod, 27 g Carb, 2 g Fib, 15 g Prot, 63 mg Calc. *POINTS* value: *5.*

For a pretty presentation, serve the salad on whole radicchio leaves. You'll need at least 2 leaves per serving, so you'll probably want to add a second head of radicchio to your shopping list.

# No-Guilt Fish and Chips

**MAKES 4 SERVINGS**

Crispy, low–**POINTS** value fish and chips without frying? You bet! Coating the fish with cornmeal and baking it in a hot oven with the potatoes is the trick. For an authentic British treat, serve the dish with malt vinegar.

2 **large baking potatoes, scrubbed and cut lengthwise into 16 spears each**
3 **tablespoons Old Bay seasoning**
$\frac{1}{2}$ **cup yellow cornmeal**
4 **(4-ounce) cod fillets**

**1.** Preheat the oven to 425°F. Spray the potatoes with nonstick spray. Place in a large zip-close plastic bag with 1 tablespoon of the Old Bay Seasoning; seal the bag and shake to coat. Transfer to a large baking sheet.

**2.** In the plastic bag, combine the cornmeal and the remaining 2 tablespoons of Old Bay; shake to mix. Spray the fish fillets with nonstick spray and place in the bag; shake to coat. Place in a single layer on the baking sheet with the potatoes. Bake until the fish is golden brown and flakes easily and the potato spears (chips) are fork-tender, about 25 minutes.

Per serving (1 fish fillet and 8 chips): 243 Cal, 1 g Fat, 0 g Sat Fat, 49 mg Chol, 1,134 mg Sod, 33 g Carb, 3 g Fib, 24 g Prot, 25 mg Calc. **POINTS** value: **4.**

If you prefer, substitute haddock fillets for the cod. Depending on the size of your baking sheets, you may need to use two. If so, switch the baking sheets' placement about halfway through the baking time.

# Flounder en Papillote

**MAKES 4 SERVINGS**

A great way to get a lot of flavor without a hefty *POINTS* value is by cooking foods en papillote, or in a parchment-paper parcel. The parchment puffs up as the food cooks and will surely impress guests when you entertain. For less glorious occasions, feel free to use foil instead of parchment paper.

1 teaspoon olive oil
1 large carrot, cut into matchstick-size pieces
1 leek, white part only, cleaned and thinly sliced
1 tomato, chopped
1 tablespoon chopped fresh thyme
1 garlic clove, minced
¼ teaspoon salt
4 (4-ounce) flounder fillets
¼ cup dry white wine

**1.** Heat the oil in a nonstick skillet over medium-low heat. Add the carrot, leek, tomato, thyme, garlic, and salt and cook, stirring frequently, until the vegetables are very tender, about 10 minutes. Remove from the heat; set aside.

**2.** Preheat the oven to 425°F.

**3.** Fold 4 (12 x 16-inch) sheets parchment paper in half. Starting at the folded edge, cut each parchment into a half-heart shape. Unfold and spray the parchment paper with nonstick spray.

**4.** Arrange the fish on half of each piece of parchment. Top with the vegetable mixture. Sprinkle with the wine. Fold the parchment into packets over the fish and vegetables, rolling the edges to make a tight seal. Place the parchment parcels on a baking sheet and bake until they are puffy and browned and the flounder is just opaque in the center, about 8 minutes.

Per serving (1 parcel): 132 Cal, 3 g Fat, 0 g Sat Fat, 56 mg Chol, 247 mg Sod, 6 g Carb, 2 g Fib, 21 g Prot, 37 mg Calc. *POINTS* value: *2.*

ready, set, five!

**COOK TO COOK** Parchment parcels are traditionally made in heart shapes, but you can use 14-inch squares of parchment. Fill them, gather the edges to make a pouch, and tie the neck with string.

# Seared Mahi Mahi with Zesty Tomato Sauce

**MAKES 4 SERVINGS**

Also called dolphinfish or dorado, mahi mahi is found in warm waters throughout the world and is commonly available on these shores as fillets or steaks. An assertive tomato-anchovy sauce complements the full flavor of the fish.

2½ teaspoons olive oil
1 scallion, sliced
1 large garlic clove, minced
½ tablespoon anchovy paste
2 tomatoes, seeded
  and chopped
2 tablespoons red-wine
  vinegar
1 tablespoon chopped
  flat-leaf parsley
4 (6-ounce) skin-on
  mahi mahi fillets
1 teaspoon coarse salt
½ teaspoon coarsely ground
  black pepper

**1.** Heat 1½ teaspoons of the oil in a small skillet over medium heat. Add the scallion and garlic and cook, stirring, until the scallion is softened. Stir in the anchovy paste and tomatoes. Increase the heat slightly and cook until thickened, about 4 minutes. Stir in the vinegar and parsley and cook 1 minute longer.

**2.** Rub both sides of the mahi mahi fillets with the remaining 1 teaspoon of oil. Season the skinless sides with the salt and pepper. Heat a nonstick skillet over medium-high heat. Put the fillets in the pan, skin-side up, and sear until browned, about 2 minutes. Turn them over and sear the other side until browned, about 2 minutes longer. Cover, reduce the heat to medium, and cook until the fish is just opaque in the center, about 3 minutes. Peel off the skin and serve the fillets drizzled with the tomato sauce.

Per serving (1 fillet with about 3 tablespoons sauce): 189 Cal, 4 g Fat, 1 g Sat Fat, 131 mg Chol, 746 mg Sod, 3 g Carb, 1 g Fib, 32 g Prot, 34 mg Calc. *POINTS* value: *4.*

Make sure to buy fillets with skin, which will keep the fish from falling apart as it cooks, then peel off the skin before serving.

meals in minutes

# Lemon Cod with Spinach-and-Potato Stew

**MAKES 4 SERVINGS**

This one-skillet dish of seared cod, simmered in a light stew of potatoes and fresh spinach with a hint of lemon, boasts a complex, delicious flavor. It's surprisingly simple to prepare, making it a perfect weeknight standby recipe.

1 pound cod fillet, cut into 4 pieces
$\frac{1}{2}$ teaspoon salt
$\frac{1}{4}$ teaspoon freshly ground pepper
3 teaspoons olive oil
1 onion, thinly sliced
1 garlic clove, minced
1 tomato, chopped
1 pound red potatoes, unpeeled, scrubbed, and quartered
$2\frac{1}{2}$ cups low-sodium chicken broth
2 teaspoons grated lemon zest
1 tablespoon fresh lemon juice
2 tablespoons cold water
1 tablespoon all-purpose flour
$\frac{1}{2}$ (10-ounce) bag baby spinach

1. Sprinkle both sides of the cod with the salt and pepper. Heat 1 teaspoon of the oil in a large nonstick skillet over medium-high heat. Add the cod and cook until it is just opaque in the center and browned on the outside, about 3 minutes on each side. Transfer to a plate; set aside.

2. Heat the remaining 2 teaspoons oil in the same skillet, then add the onion and garlic. Cook over medium-low heat, stirring occasionally, until the onion is very tender, about 8 minutes. Add the tomato; cook until soft, about 5 minutes. Add the potatoes, broth, lemon zest, and lemon juice; bring to a boil. Reduce the heat and simmer, covered, until potatoes are fork-tender, about 15 minutes.

3. Meanwhile, whisk together the water and flour in a small bowl until smooth. Stir mixture into the simmering vegetables. Add the spinach. Cook, stirring constantly, until the sauce thickens and the spinach begins to wilt, 2–3 minutes. Return the cod to the skillet; heat through.

Per serving (1 piece cod and $1\frac{1}{4}$ cups stew): 282 Cal, 6 g Fat, 1 g Sat Fat, 60 mg Chol, 459 mg Sod, 31 g Carb, 4 g Fib, 27 g Prot, 77 mg Calc. **POINTS** value: **5.**

ready, set, five!

# Asian Steak and Noodles

**MAKES 6 SERVINGS**

Even if you typically avoid spicy ingredients like pepper flakes, don't omit them here; a small amount is needed to balance the sweetness of the hoisin and the sharpness of the ginger. Of course, if you prefer a spicier dish, increase the red pepper to ½ teaspoon.

2½ tablespoons reduced-
   sodium soy sauce
1 tablespoon dry sherry
½ teaspoon grated peeled
   fresh ginger
1 garlic clove, minced
1 pound flank steak,
   trimmed of all visible fat
1 (8-ounce) package
   lo mein noodles
2 tablespoons hoisin sauce
1 teaspoon Asian (dark)
   sesame oil
⅛ teaspoon crushed red
   pepper, or to taste
1 red bell pepper, seeded
   and thinly sliced
1 green bell pepper, seeded
   and thinly sliced
2 scallions, thinly sliced

**1.** In a shallow baking dish, mix 1 tablespoon of the soy sauce, the sherry, ginger, and garlic. Add the steak, turning to coat. Let stand 20 minutes to marinate.

**2.** Meanwhile, cook the noodles according to package directions; drain and transfer to a large bowl. Toss with the remaining 1½ tablespoons soy sauce, the hoisin sauce, sesame oil, and crushed red pepper. Then add the bell peppers and scallions; toss to combine.

**3.** Spray a broiler rack with nonstick spray; preheat the broiler. Broil the steak 5 inches from the heat until an instant-read thermometer inserted into the center of the steak registers 160°F for medium, 145°F for medium-rare, about 4 minutes on each side for medium. Thinly slice the steak on the diagonal across the grain into about 24 slices. Divide the noodles and vegetables among 6 plates; top with the steak slices.

Per serving (4 slices steak and ¾ cup noodles and vegetables): 244 Cal, 9 g Fat, 4 g Sat Fat, 51 mg Chol, 376 mg Sod, 17 g Carb, 3 g Fib, 24 g Prot, 31 mg Calc. **POINTS** value: **5.**

*ready, set, five!*

Look for lo mein noodles in your supermarket's Asian-food section; if you can't find them, use soba noodles or fettuccine.

# Roasted Sea Bass with Tomato Coulis

**MAKES 4 SERVINGS**

Don't be afraid to roast a whole fish—it's so easy! Simply seasoned, this dish derives much of its rich smoky flavor from the Marsala in the coulis (a French term for thick puree or sauce). But you can also substitute dry white wine or water for the Marsala.

1 (1¼–1½-pound) whole striped bass, cleaned
¼ teaspoon salt
¼ teaspoon coarsely ground black pepper
3 basil sprigs
1 tablespoon olive oil
1 large white onion, chopped
3 large garlic cloves, chopped
⅓ cup chopped fresh basil
¼ cup dry Marsala
2 tomatoes, peeled, seeded, and roughly chopped

**1.** Preheat the oven to 450°F. Spray a baking sheet with nonstick spray.

**2.** Sprinkle the cavity of the fish with the salt and pepper, then put the basil sprigs into the cavity. Place the fish on the baking sheet and spray top of the fish with nonstick spray. Roast 8 minutes, spray the top again, and roast until the fish is just opaque in the center, 12–14 minutes longer.

**3.** Meanwhile, heat the oil in a large nonstick skillet over medium-high heat. Add the onion and cook, stirring, until it begins to soften and turn translucent, about 5 minutes. Stir in the garlic and cook until fragrant. Stir in the chopped basil and the Marsala and cook 1 minute longer, then stir in the tomatoes. Cook, uncovered, stirring occasionally, until the tomatoes break down into a thick, chunky sauce, about 20 minutes. Fillet the fish and divide among 4 dinner plates. Serve topped with the coulis.

Per serving (¼ fish with ½ cup coulis): 245 Cal, 8 g Fat, 1 g Sat Fat, 136 mg Chol, 270 mg Sod, 8 g Carb, 1 g Fib, 31 g Prot, 45 mg Calc. **POINTS** value: *5.*

When you're preparing a whole fish, here's an easy way to determine when it is perfectly cooked: Gently pull on the fin in the center of the fish's back. When the fin pulls away easily, the fish is done. (You can also check that the flesh is just opaque in the center.)

meals in minutes

# Herb-Marinated Steak and Vegetables

**MAKES 4 SERVINGS**

Boneless New York strip steak, also called Kansas City steak, is an excellent cut of beef for broiling or grilling. Juicy and flavorful but firm enough for marinating, it's particularly tasty when marinated with fresh basil and red wine.

$^3/_4$ cup dry red wine

$^1/_4$ cup chopped fresh basil

2 (6-ounce) New York strip steaks, trimmed of all visible fat

$^1/_2$ tablespoon olive oil

1 yellow onion, sliced

1 red bell pepper, seeded and sliced

1 (10-ounce) bag triple-washed spinach, rinsed and chopped

$^1/_4$ teaspoon salt

$^1/_4$ teaspoon coarsely ground black pepper

1 teaspoon balsamic vinegar

**1.** Combine the wine and basil in a zip-close plastic bag, then add the steaks. Squeeze out the air and seal the bag; turn to coat the steaks. Refrigerate, turning the bag occasionally, 1–2 hours.

**2.** Spray a broiler rack with nonstick spray; preheat the broiler. Remove the steaks from the marinade and pat dry. Broil the steaks 5 inches from the heat until an instant-read thermometer inserted into the center of each steak registers 160°F for medium, 145°F for medium-rare, 3–4 minutes on each side for medium.

**3.** Heat the oil in a nonstick skillet over medium-high heat. Add the onion and bell pepper and cook, stirring, until the onion is golden brown. Add the spinach, then the salt and black pepper; cook until wilted, about 1 minute. Stir in the vinegar and remove from the heat. Thinly slice the steak and layer slices over the vegetables.

Per serving (4 slices steak and $^3/_4$ cup vegetables): 234 Cal, 13 g Fat, 5 g Sat Fat, 43 mg Chol, 238 mg Sod, 7 g Carb, 3 g Fib, 15 g Prot, 89 mg Calc. *POINTS* value: *5.*

**COOK TO COOK**

Don't marinate the steaks longer than recommended or the marinade will begin to break down the fibers of the meat, making it tough and chewy. Heat the broiler well to promote browning, and only open it once to turn the steaks over, so as not to lower the broiler temperature.

*ready, set, five!*

# Pork Tenderloin with Plum Chutney

**MAKES 4 SERVINGS**

This spectacular dish is extraordinarily flavorful, elegant, and easy to prepare. Although this chutney features such traditional ingredients as vinegar, brown sugar, ginger, and dry mustard, it's a chunkier and fresher rendition than most long-cooked chutneys. Compliment this beautiful dish with a colorful rice-and-peppers pilaf.

$\frac{1}{3}$ cup apple cider vinegar

2 scallions, sliced

3 tablespoons packed light brown sugar

$\frac{1}{2}$ tablespoon grated peeled fresh ginger

$\frac{1}{2}$ teaspoon dry mustard

5 ripe plums, pitted and cut into 1-inch chunks

3 tablespoons Italian-style dried bread crumbs

1 tablespoon pine nuts

1 ($\frac{3}{4}$-pound) pork tenderloin, trimmed of all visible fat

2 teaspoons Dijon mustard

**1.** Preheat the oven to 475°F. Bring the vinegar, scallions, brown sugar, ginger, and dry mustard to a boil in a medium skillet over medium heat. Boil to form a syrup, 4–5 minutes. Stir in the plums, reduce the heat to low, and cook until the plums are soft and well glazed, about 10 minutes. Transfer to a bowl to cool.

**2.** Meanwhile, combine the bread crumbs and pine nuts in a food processor or blender and grind to a fine consistency. Transfer the mixture to a plate or a sheet of wax paper. Rub the tenderloin all over with the Dijon mustard, then roll in the bread crumb mixture to coat and set in a baking dish. Roast until the pork reaches an internal temperature of 160°F, 20–25 minutes. Remove from the oven and let stand 10 minutes before slicing. Serve with the chutney on the side.

Per serving (3 slices pork with about $\frac{1}{2}$ cup chutney): 226 Cal, 5 g Fat, 1 g Sat Fat, 55 mg Chol, 195 mg Sod, 26 g Carb, 2 g Fib, 20 g Prot, 32 mg Calc. **POINTS** value: **5.**

 Try to use red plums for the chutney, to achieve a beautiful jewel-like color. Black plums will still be tasty, but their darker skin isn't quite as pretty.

*meals in minutes*

Pork Tenderloin
with Plum Chutney

# Country-Style Lamb and Barley Stew

**MAKES 6 SERVINGS**

Stews are often better the next day, when spices have mingled and flavors have had a chance to develop—and this recipe, scented with fresh rosemary, is no exception. If you make it a day ahead and refrigerate it, the stew will be rich and robust by the time you serve it. Adding lots of veggies to each serving keeps the *POINTS* value in check.

1 teaspoon olive oil

1 pound lean lamb cubes
  for stew, trimmed of
  all visible fat

1 onion, chopped

2 garlic cloves, minced

1 tablespoon tomato paste

1 tablespoon chopped
  fresh rosemary

6 cups low-sodium
  chicken broth

½ cup pearl barley, rinsed

2 carrots, cut into
  ¼-inch slices

½ pound green beans,
  trimmed and cut into
  1-inch pieces

1 (9-ounce) package frozen
  pearl onions

1 cup frozen peas

1. Heat the oil in a large nonstick saucepan over medium-high heat. Add the lamb and cook until browned on all sides, about 6 minutes. Add the onion and garlic. Cook, stirring frequently, until the onion is softened, about 5 minutes. Stir in the tomato paste and rosemary until blended. Add the broth and barley; bring to a boil. Reduce the heat and simmer, covered, until the lamb and barley are tender, about 40 minutes.

2. Add the carrots, beans, and pearl onions. Simmer, uncovered, until vegetables are tender, about 6 minutes. Stir in the peas; heat through.

Per serving (1⅓ cups): 245 Cal, 6 g Fat, 2 g Sat Fat, 42 mg Chol, 143 mg Sod, 28 g Carb, 7 g Fib, 20 g Prot, 61 mg Calc. *POINTS* value: *5.*

**meals in minutes**

# Southwestern Ham, Cheese, and Potato Casserole

**MAKES 4 SERVINGS**

Leaving the skins on the potatoes adds a touch of extra fiber to this recipe, while a generous amount of red and green bell peppers contributes a nice vitamin boost. A simple green salad will complete the meal.

1 teaspoon olive oil

1 red bell pepper, seeded and chopped

1 green bell pepper, seeded and chopped

1 bunch scallions, thinly sliced

1 cup cherry tomatoes, quartered

1/4 pound sliced cooked ham, cut into strips

2 teaspoons chili powder

2 teaspoons ground cumin

1/2 teaspoon freshly ground pepper

2 baking potatoes, scrubbed and thinly sliced

1/2 cup shredded reduced-fat cheddar cheese

1. Preheat the oven to 350°F. Spray an 8-inch-square baking dish with nonstick spray.

2. Heat the oil in a large nonstick skillet over medium-high heat. Add the red and green bell peppers and scallions and cook, stirring occasionally, until softened, about 5 minutes. Add the tomatoes, ham, chili powder, cumin, and ground pepper; cook until heated through, about 2 minutes.

3. Spread half of the potatoes in the baking dish, top with half of the bell pepper mixture. Repeat layering once more. Cover with foil and bake until the potatoes are tender, about 45 minutes. Uncover, sprinkle with the cheese, and bake until the cheese is lightly browned, about 10 minutes longer.

Per serving (1/4 of casserole): 231 Cal, 7 g Fat, 3 g Sat Fat, 24 mg Chol, 531 mg Sod, 30 g Carb, 5 g Fib, 14 g Prot, 156 mg Calc. *POINTS* value: *4.*

ready, set, five!

Torta de Fideua

# Torta de Fideua

**MAKES 4 SERVINGS**

Tortas, or open-face omelettes, are a popular bar food in Spain because they hold up well at room temperature. So they're also perfect for a buffet. Use any cooked pasta in this dish; if using long noodles, roughly chop them. For a dramatic presentation, bring the torta to the table in the heavy (preferably cast-iron) skillet in which it is baked.

1 small red bell pepper, seeded and sliced

1 small Vidalia onion, sliced

1 garlic clove, minced

2 large eggs

½ cup fat-free egg substitute

⅓ cup fat-free milk

2 tablespoons reduced-fat sour cream

1 cup chopped cooked pasta

½ cup diced turkey ham

2 tablespoons thinly sliced fresh basil

1 teaspoon paprika

¾ teaspoon salt

¼ teaspoon coarsely ground black pepper

⅛ teaspoon cayenne

**1.** Preheat the oven to 325°F. Spray a heavy medium skillet (with an ovenproof handle) with nonstick spray and set over medium-high heat. Add the bell pepper, onion, and garlic and cook until the onions are lightly browned and the bell peppers are soft. Transfer to a bowl and set aside. Put the skillet into the oven to keep hot.

**2.** Whisk together the eggs, egg substitute, milk, sour cream, pasta, turkey ham, basil, paprika, salt, pepper, and cayenne. Stir in the vegetables. Pour the mixture into the skillet and bake until the edges are set and the torta is lightly browned, about 25 minutes.

Per serving (¼ torta): 145 Cal, 4 g Fat, 2 g Sat Fat, 120 mg Chol, 689 mg Sod, 15 g Carb, 1 g Fib, 12 g Prot, 83 mg Calc. **POINTS** value: **3.**

To cut basil leaves into thin strips, stack leaves of similar size. Roll them into a cigar shape, then slice. If your skillet's handle is not ovenproof, cover handle with heavy-duty foil before baking.

# in a jiffy

BIG-ON-FLAVOR RECIPES THAT ARE
SHORT ON COOKING TIME

# Italian Bread Soup with Escarole

**MAKES 4 SERVINGS**

Pancetta, a flavorful Italian bacon in a sausagelike shape, makes this soup taste like it has simmered for hours instead of just a matter of minutes. Tightly wrapped, it keeps in the refrigerator for up to three weeks and in the freezer for up to six months.

2 tablespoons chopped pancetta
1 onion, chopped
3 garlic cloves, minced
4 cups low-sodium vegetable or chicken broth
1 (14-ounce) can Italian plum tomatoes
1 bunch escarole, chopped (about 5 cups)
1½ tablespoons chopped fresh oregano, or 1½ teaspoons dried
½ teaspoon freshly ground pepper
2 (15-ounce) cans cannellini (white kidney) beans, rinsed and drained
4 ounces Italian bread, cut into 8 slices
⅓ cup shredded Parmesan cheese

1. Spray a nonstick Dutch oven with nonstick spray and set over medium heat. Add the pancetta and cook until browned, 2–3 minutes; transfer to a plate.

2. Add the onion and garlic to the same Dutch oven. Cook, stirring frequently, until golden, 7–10 minutes. Add the broth, tomatoes, escarole, oregano, and pepper; bring to a boil, stirring occasionally. Reduce the heat and simmer, covered, until the escarole is softened, about 5 minutes. Stir in the beans and cook until the soup is hot, 2–3 minutes.

3. Preheat the broiler. Transfer the soup to a large ovenproof casserole dish. Arrange the bread slices on top of the soup; sprinkle with the cheese. Broil until the cheese and bread are lightly browned, 1–2 minutes. Sprinkle with the pancetta just before serving.

Per serving (generous 2 cups): 385 Cal, 6 g Fat, 2 g Sat Fat, 7 mg Chol, 910 mg Sod, 62 g Carb, 16 g Fib, 23 g Prot, 275 mg Calc.
*POINTS* value: *7.*

**COOK TO COOK** To save even more time, use a 10-ounce package of frozen chopped spinach, thawed and squeezed dry, in place of the fresh escarole, and broil the soup right in the Dutch oven. Just remember to cover nonflameproof handles with heavy-duty foil to prevent them from scorching.

# Quick Jalapeño Corn Soup

**MAKES 6 SERVINGS**

Thanks to quick-cooking corn and diced red potatoes, this south-of-the-border chowder is ready in a snap. The amount of corn you can scrape from the ear varies considerably—you'll get between 1/2 and 1 1/4 cups, depending on its size. Feel free to substitute frozen corn kernels. For a spicier soup, use a whole jalapeño.

2 teaspoons olive oil
1 onion, chopped
2 garlic cloves, minced
2 1/2 cups corn kernels
2 red potatoes, peeled and diced
1/2 jalapeño pepper, seeded and chopped (wear gloves to prevent irritation)
3 cups low-sodium chicken broth
1/4 teaspoon salt
1/4 teaspoon freshly ground pepper
1/2 red bell pepper, seeded and diced
1 tablespoon chopped fresh cilantro

**1.** Heat the oil in a large nonstick saucepan over medium-high heat. Add the onion and cook, stirring occasionally, until softened and beginning to brown, about 3 minutes. Add the garlic and stir 15 seconds. Stir in the corn, potatoes, and jalapeño; cook, stirring, until the corn begins to soften, about 3 minutes. Add the broth; bring to a boil. Reduce the heat to low and simmer, covered, until the vegetables can be easily mashed, about 15 minutes.
**2.** Transfer to a food processor or blender, add the salt and pepper, and puree. Serve, sprinkled with the bell pepper and cilantro.

Per serving (about 3/4 cup): 125 Cal, 3 g Fat, 1 g Sat Fat, 3 mg Chol, 157 mg Sod, 24 g Carb, 3 g Fib, 5 g Prot, 23 mg Calc. *POINTS* value: *2.*

**COOK TO COOK** If you prefer a chunkier soup, puree half of the mixture and stir it back into the pot before seasoning with salt and pepper.

in a jiffy

# Speedy Cock-a-Leekie

**MAKES 4 SERVINGS**

This soothing Scottish brew translates as "chicken and leeks." Prunes are traditionally added for a touch of sweetness, but the sweetest thing of all is that this soup can be on the table in 20 minutes. Compliment each bowlful with a slice of oat-bran bread, toasted and cut into triangles (and increase the per-serving *POINTS* value by 2).

1 teaspoon canola oil
1¼ pounds leeks, thinly sliced
6 cups low-sodium chicken broth
⅔ cup quick-cooking barley
2 parsnips, finely chopped
½ teaspoon freshly ground pepper
¾ pound skinless boneless chicken breasts, cut into 1-inch pieces
½ pound white mushrooms, sliced
6 pitted prunes, chopped
1 teaspoon dried thyme
2 tablespoons port or dry sherry

**1.** Heat the oil in a nonstick Dutch oven over medium heat. Add the leeks and cook, stirring occasionally, until softened, 7–8 minutes. Add the broth, barley, parsnips, and pepper; bring to a boil. Reduce the heat and simmer, covered, about 8 minutes.

**2.** Add the chicken, mushrooms, prunes, and thyme; return to a boil. Reduce the heat and simmer, covered, until the chicken is just cooked through, 3–4 minutes. Stir in the port or sherry.

Per serving (generous 2 cups): 387 Cal, 6 g Fat, 1 g Sat Fat, 46 mg Chol, 149 mg Sod, 55 g Carb, 11 g Fib, 29 g Prot, 115 mg Calc. *POINTS* value: *7.*

Here's how to clean often-sandy leeks: Trim away most of the dark-green tops and the roots, leaving the root end intact to hold the layers together. Slice the leek lengthwise to a half inch from the root end. Hold by the root end, fan open the layers, and rinse thoroughly under cold running water.

# Chicken and Crab Gumbo

**MAKES 6 SERVINGS**

Here's a quick version of gumbo that starts with a dry roux rather than the usual fat-laden roux made with tons of oil. The darker the flour becomes when you toast it, the richer the gumbo will be—but take care not to let it burn.

$\frac{1}{4}$ cup all-purpose flour

$\frac{1}{2}$ tablespoon canola oil

1 white onion, chopped

1 red bell pepper, seeded and chopped

1 celery stalk, chopped

3 garlic cloves, chopped

$\frac{1}{4}$ teaspoon cayenne

1 bay leaf

$\frac{3}{4}$ pound skinless boneless chicken breast, cubed

4 cups chicken broth

$\frac{1}{2}$ pound cooked fresh or frozen crabmeat, picked over

1 tablespoon filé powder

3 cups cooked white rice

**1.** In a small heavy saucepan, cook the flour over medium-high heat, stirring constantly with a wooden spoon, until it turns dark tan, 3–4 minutes. Remove from the heat and set aside.

**2.** Heat the oil in a nonstick Dutch oven over medium-high heat. Add the onion, bell pepper, celery, and garlic and cook, stirring, until the onion is softened. Stir in the flour, then add the cayenne, bay leaf, and chicken. Still stirring, add the broth and crabmeat and bring to a boil. Cover, reduce the heat, and simmer until thickened and the chicken is cooked through, about 20 minutes.

**3.** Discard the bay leaf and stir in the filé powder. Put $\frac{1}{2}$ cup rice in each of 6 large, shallow bowls and ladle the gumbo on top.

Per serving (about 1$\frac{1}{2}$ cups gumbo and $\frac{1}{2}$ cup rice): 295 Cal, 5 g Fat, 1 g Sat Fat, 48 mg Chol, 764 mg Sod, 38 g Carb, 1 g Fib, 23 g Prot, 27 mg Calc. **POINTS** value: **6.**

*in a jiffy*

**COOK TO COOK**

Filé powder, a Creole spice, is made from sassafras leaves. It adds a woodsy accent and thickens the gumbo. It can become stringy and tough if cooked too long or over too high a heat, so it's typically stirred in at the end of cooking.

# Pasta Salad Tonnato

**MAKES 6 SERVINGS**

This main-dish pasta salad, made with tuna, olives, and capers, is ideal for a summer luncheon, a quick supper, or an easy picnic. It all comes together in a snap with just a few simple staples from your kitchen pantry. If you're a salmon fan, feel free to substitute canned salmon for the tuna.

8 ounces penne pasta

1 (12-ounce) can water-packed chunk light tuna, drained

3 celery stalks, finely chopped

½ red onion, thinly sliced

10 kalamata olives, pitted and chopped

2 tablespoons capers, drained and chopped

2 teaspoons grated lemon zest

⅓ cup reduced-calorie mayonnaise

2 tablespoons Dijon mustard

1 tablespoon fresh lemon juice

Pinch cayenne

**1.** Cook the penne according to package directions, then drain and rinse under cold running water. Transfer the penne to a large bowl. Add the tuna, celery, onion, olives, capers, and lemon zest.

**2.** Whisk together the mayonnaise, mustard, lemon juice, and cayenne until blended. Stir the mayonnaise mixture with the pasta mixture until blended.

Per serving (1 cup): 268 Cal, 7 g Fat, 1 g Sat Fat, 20 mg Chol, 490 mg Sod, 33 g Carb, 2 g Fib, 19 g Prot, 35 mg Calc. *POINTS* value: *6.*

**COOK TO COOK** Make this salad extra-filling—and extra-colorful—by serving it on a bed of vibrant greens and topping it off with sliced cherry tomatoes.

Pasta Salad Tonnato

# Gnocchi Marinara

**MAKES 4 SERVINGS**

High-quality, premade gnocchi is now available in many supermarkets; look for it near the dried pastas. It comes in a variety of flavors and cooks in just 3 to 4 minutes.

1 (16-ounce) package gnocchi
2 teaspoons olive oil
1 onion, chopped
3 garlic cloves, peeled
2 tomatoes, peeled, seeded and chopped
1/4 cup chopped fresh basil
Pinch crushed red pepper
2 tablespoons grated Parmesan cheese

**1.** Cook the gnocchi according to package directions. Drain and keep warm.

**2.** Meanwhile, heat the oil in a nonstick skillet over medium heat. Add the onion and cook, stirring, until golden, about 5 minutes. Press in the garlic with a garlic press, then add the tomatoes, basil, and red pepper. Cook until the tomatoes have broken down to form a thick sauce, about 20 minutes. Add the gnocchi; toss to coat. Serve at once, sprinkled with the cheese.

Per serving (scant 1 cup): 252 Cal, 17 g Fat, 6 g Sat Fat, 81 mg Chol, 360 mg Sod, 14 g Carb, 1 g Fib, 12 g Prot, 278 mg Calc. *POINTS* value: *6.*

This is a good, basic tomato sauce that works with any variety of pasta. Try it with a chunky shape like shells or radiatore, or serve it with polenta.

*meals in minutes*

# Chicken Pepper Steak with Hash Browns

**MAKES 4 SERVINGS**

Seasoned pepper blend is a combination of coarse-ground black pepper and sweet bell peppers. It suffuses the chicken with spiciness and a touch of sweetness in this simple dish. Substitute a Szechuan-style pepper blend if you want to turn up the heat even more. A green salad tossed with green apple slices makes a refreshing accompaniment.

1 teaspoon grated lime zest

2 tablespoons fresh
lime juice

2 garlic cloves, minced

4 (4-ounce) skinless
boneless chicken breasts

2 teaspoons canola oil

4 cups (from a 32-ounce
bag) frozen hash-brown
potatoes

$\frac{1}{2}$ teaspoon salt

3 tablespoons chopped
fresh parsley

2 tablespoons seasoned
pepper blend (no
salt added)

1. Combine the lime zest, lime juice, and garlic in a zip-close plastic bag; add the chicken. Squeeze out the air and seal the bag; turn to coat the chicken. Let stand 10 minutes.

2. Meanwhile, heat the oil in a large nonstick skillet over medium-high heat. Add the potatoes and salt and cook, stirring frequently, until the potatoes are tender and lightly browned, about 10 minutes. Stir in the parsley.

3. Spread the pepper blend on wax paper. Remove the chicken from the marinade (discard the marinade) and lightly press into the pepper, coating both sides.

4. Spray a nonstick skillet or a nonstick ridged grill pan with nonstick spray and set over medium heat. Add the chicken and cook until it is lightly browned and just cooked through, 4–5 minutes on each side. Serve with the hash browns.

Per serving (1 chicken breast and $^3/_4$ cup hash browns): 338 Cal, 6 g Fat, 1 g Sat Fat, 62 mg Chol, 400 mg Sod, 43 g Carb, 5 g Fib, 28 g Prot, 47 mg Calc. **POINTS** value: **6.**

in a jiffy

**Honey-Ginger
Chicken with
Orange Rice**

# Honey-Ginger Chicken with Orange Rice

**MAKES 4 SERVINGS**

Honey-dipped chicken breasts, coated in a savory blend of pecans and cornmeal, are the star attraction of this down-home dish. For a more even coating, after you've rolled the chicken breasts in the cornmeal mixture, spread the mixture with a knife.

$1\frac{1}{3}$ cups water

$\frac{2}{3}$ cup orange juice

1 cup long-grain rice

1 tablespoon chopped fresh parsley

1 teaspoon grated orange zest

$\frac{1}{2}$ cup pecan halves

$\frac{1}{4}$ cup white cornmeal

$\frac{1}{4}$ teaspoon freshly ground pepper

1 tablespoon honey

$\frac{1}{2}$ tablespoon reduced-sodium soy sauce

$\frac{1}{2}$ teaspoon grated peeled fresh ginger

4 (4-ounce) skinless boneless chicken breasts

**1.** In a medium saucepan, combine the water and orange juice; bring to a boil. Stir in the rice; reduce the heat and simmer, covered, until the liquid is absorbed and the rice is tender, about 15 minutes. Fluff with a fork, then stir in the parsley and orange zest.

**2.** Meanwhile, spray a broiler rack with nonstick spray; preheat the broiler.

**3.** In a food processor, combine the pecans, cornmeal, and pepper until the nuts are finely ground. Transfer to a plate. In a shallow bowl, combine the honey, soy sauce, and ginger. Dip the chicken in the honey mixture, then roll it in the cornmeal mixture.

**4.** Broil the chicken 5 inches from the heat until crusty brown and cooked through, about 4 minutes on each side. Serve with the rice.

Per serving (1 chicken breast and about $\frac{3}{4}$ cup rice): 335 Cal, 11 g Fat, 1 g Sat Fat, 66 mg Chol, 142 mg Sod, 29 g Carb, 2 g Fib, 30 g Prot, 30 mg Calc. **POINTS** value: **7.**

*in a jiffy*

**COOK TO COOK** White cornmeal is a better choice than yellow when broiling; yellow is quicker to burn under direct heat, while white browns better. A small amount of nuts adds wonderful flavor and richness with only a little fat. If you prefer to avoid nuts, however, use wheat-and-barley cereal nuggets instead.

# Cajun-Style Monkfish

**MAKES 4 SERVINGS**

Monkfish is a low-fat, firm-textured fish with a mild, sweet taste. As an homage to you-know-who, we "kicked the flavor up a notch" with Cajun seasoning and a garlicky tomato sauce. Cooked brown rice makes a perfect accompaniment to this dish.

1 **pound monkfish fillets, cut into 4 pieces**

2 **tablespoons Cajun seasoning**

1 **tablespoon olive oil**

2 **green bell peppers, seeded and thinly sliced**

1 **large onion, thinly sliced**

2 **garlic cloves, minced**

1 **(14¹/₂-ounce) can stewed tomatoes**

1 **tablespoon chopped fresh thyme, or 1 teaspoon dried**

**1.** Sprinkle the fish with 1 tablespoon of the Cajun seasoning. Heat 1 teaspoon of the oil in a large nonstick skillet over medium-high heat. Add the fish and cook until browned, about 3 minutes on each side. Transfer the fish to a plate; set aside.

**2.** Heat the remaining 2 teaspoons oil in the same skillet, then add the bell peppers, onion, garlic, and the remaining 1 tablespoon Cajun seasoning. Cook over medium heat, stirring occasionally, until the vegetables are very tender, about 8 minutes. Add the tomatoes with their liquid, and the thyme; bring to a boil. Return the monkfish to the skillet. Reduce the heat and simmer, covered, until the flavors are blended and the fish is opaque in the center, about 8 minutes.

Per serving (1 monkfish fillet and 1 cup sauce): 196 Cal, 5 g Fat, 1 g Sat Fat, 62 mg Chol, 1,144 mg Sod, 14 g Carb, 2 g Fib, 24 g Prot, 65 mg Calc. ***POINTS*** value: ***4.***

meals in minutes

# Mussels with Garlic, Tomatoes, and Wine

**MAKES 4 SERVINGS**

One scent of these mussels in their aromatic broth and you'll be transported to a little fishing village in the Mediterranean. Serve with crusty bread to sop up the juices.

1 tablespoon olive oil
3 shallots, thinly sliced
3 garlic cloves, minced
1 tablespoon chopped
   fresh thyme
6 plum tomatoes, chopped
2 pounds mussels,
   scrubbed and debearded
1½ cups low-sodium
   chicken broth
½ cup dry white wine
¼ cup chopped fresh basil

**1.** Heat the oil in a large nonstick saucepan over medium heat. Add the shallots, garlic, and thyme and cook, stirring occasionally, until the shallots are softened, about 3 minutes. Add the tomatoes and cook until soft and the flavors are blended, about 8 minutes. Stir in the mussels, broth, and wine; bring to a boil, stirring occasionally. Reduce the heat and simmer, covered, until the mussels have opened, about 5 minutes. Discard any mussels that do not open.

**2.** Transfer the mussels to 4 bowls; stir the basil into the broth, then pour over the mussels.

Per serving (about 12 mussels and ½ cup broth): 148 Cal, 5 g Fat, 1 g Sat Fat, 34 mg Chol, 92 mg Sod, 10 g Carb, 2 g Fib, 15 g Prot, 81 mg Calc. *POINTS* value: **3.**

in a jiffy

When purchasing mussels, look for tightly closed shells or shells that close when lightly tapped. Scrub them with a stiff brush under cold running water to remove any sand. Discard any mussels that remain open. To debeard, pinch the hairy filaments between thumb and forefinger and pull firmly.

**Creamy Fettuccine with Scallops and Spinach**

# Creamy Fettuccine with Scallops and Spinach

**MAKES 4 SERVINGS**

For a nice variation and a pretty color contrast, try this with carrot or tomato fettuccine instead of the plain variety. The elegant sauce boasts portobello mushrooms, sautéed with a touch of soy sauce to bring out their woodsy flavor.

½ pound fettuccine

2 tablespoons all-purpose flour

½ teaspoon salt

¼ teaspoon ground nutmeg

2 cups low-fat (1%) milk

2 teaspoons olive oil

¾ pound sea scallops, patted dry and muscle tabs removed

6 ounces portobello mushrooms, sliced (about 2 cups)

1 shallot, finely chopped

1 tablespoon reduced-sodium soy sauce

2 pounds spinach, coarsely chopped

1. Cook the fettuccine according to package directions. Drain and keep warm.

2. Combine the flour, salt, and nutmeg in a medium nonstick saucepan. Gradually whisk in the milk and cook over medium heat, stirring constantly, until the sauce boils and thickens, about 8 minutes. Remove the white sauce from the heat; set aside.

3. Meanwhile, heat 1 teaspoon of the oil in a large nonstick skillet over medium-high heat. Add the scallops and cook until lightly browned on the outside and just opaque in the center, about 2 minutes on each side. Transfer the scallops to a plate. Wipe the skillet clean.

4. Heat the remaining 1 teaspoon oil in the same skillet, then add the mushrooms, shallot, and soy sauce. Cook over medium heat, stirring occasionally, until the mushrooms are tender and browned, about 5 minutes. Stir in the fettuccine, white sauce, scallops, and spinach, tossing to coat well. Cook, stirring frequently, until the mixture is heated through and the spinach just wilts, about 4 minutes.

Per serving (1½ cups): 431 Cal, 8 g Fat, 2 g Sat Fat, 81 mg Chol, 870 mg Sod, 57 g Carb, 7 g Fib, 36 g Prot, 436 mg Calc. **POINTS** value: **8.**

We suggest taking a few extra minutes to nip off the too-tough-to-chew muscle tabs attached to sea scallops before cooking them. To get the scallops to brown around the edges, make sure they are patted thoroughly dry with paper towels before you sauté them.

# Salmon with Greens and Black Bean Sauce

**MAKES 4 SERVINGS**

Steaming is not only a fat-free way to cook, it's also one of the quickest methods to prepare just about anything. We steam both the salmon and kale, which keeps them super moist and delicious. An Asian green like bok choy would be nice in this, but kale's assertive flavor and brilliant color are a better foil for salmon. You could also use spinach. Look for the black bean garlic sauce in the Asian section of your supermarket.

¼ teaspoon Asian (dark) sesame oil
1 bunch kale, chopped
1 small red onion, thinly sliced
4 (6-ounce) skinless salmon fillets
¾ cup vegetable broth
1 tablespoon black bean garlic sauce
½ tablespoon cornstarch
1 teaspoon grated peeled fresh ginger

**1.** Coat a plate that will fit inside a steamer basket with the sesame oil. Put the kale onto the plate, scatter the onion over the kale, and arrange the salmon fillets on top. Place the plate into the basket over 1 inch of boiling water. Cover tightly and steam until the fish is just opaque in the center, 10–12 minutes.

**2.** Meanwhile, in a small saucepan mix the broth, black bean garlic sauce, cornstarch, and ginger; bring to a boil, stirring constantly, then boil until thick and translucent, about 2 minutes.

**3.** To serve, divide the salmon and kale among 4 plates, scattering the onion over the kale. Drizzle with the sauce.

Per serving (1 salmon fillet with ¼ of kale and sauce): 294 Cal, 8 g Fat, 0 g Sat Fat, 121 mg Chol, 855 mg Sod, 16 g Carb, 3 g Fib, 47 g Prot, 160 mg Calc. *POINTS* value: **6.**

The easiest way to steam fish fillets is to arrange them in a single layer on a dinner plate and put the plate in a flat-bottomed steamer basket, such as a bamboo Chinese steamer or the steamer insert of a Dutch oven.

meals in minutes

# Seared Tuna Steak Salad

**MAKES 4 SERVINGS**

Cooking times in this recipe will yield rare tuna, still slightly pink in the center. If you prefer your tuna done more, cook for 30 seconds (or so) longer per side. Use either ahi or yellowfin tuna.

1 teaspoon + 1 tablespoon olive oil
1 tablespoon chopped grated lemon zest
1 teaspoon coarsely ground black pepper
Pinch salt
1 (12-ounce) tuna steak
1½ tablespoons balsamic vinegar
1 tablespoon water
1 teaspoon Dijon mustard
1 teaspoon rosemary leaves
4 cups mesclun

**1.** Combine 1 teaspoon of the oil, the lemon zest, pepper, and salt in a food processor and whirl to make a paste. Rub the paste over the tuna steak.

**2.** Heat a nonstick skillet over medium-high heat. Spray one side of the tuna with nonstick spray and set the steak, sprayed-side down, in the pan. Sear until browned, about 2 minutes. Spray the top, turn the steak over, and brown the other side, about 2 minutes longer. Remove from the pan and cut into 16 slices.

**3.** To make the dressing, blend the vinegar, water, mustard, rosemary, and the remaining 1 tablespoon of the oil with a whisk or in a mini food processor.

**4.** Mound 1 cup of the mesclun on each of 4 salad plates. Fan 4 slices of tuna over the greens and drizzle with about 1 tablespoon of the dressing.

Per serving (4 slices tuna, 1 cup mesclun, and 1 tablespoon dressing): 150 Cal, 6 g Fat, 1 g Sat Fat, 38 mg Chol, 224 mg Sod, 4 g Carb, 1 g Fib, 21 g Prot, 58 mg Calc. **POINTS** value: **3.**

**COOK TO COOK** If you don't have any fresh rosemary on hand for the balsamic vinaigrette, replace with ½ teaspoon dried rosemary, crumbled.

# Cornmeal-Almond Trout

**MAKES 2 SERVINGS**

This dish sports an enticing crust—crunchy and flavored with a hint of almonds. Readily available and often inexpensive, farm-raised rainbow trout are larger and sweeter than brook trout. Make a meal of this delicious fish with steamed Yukon Gold potatoes and a summer-squash medley on the side. Pass the hot sauce at the table.

1 tablespoon blanched
   almonds
2 tablespoons cornmeal
¼ teaspoon salt + additional
   to season fish
⅛ teaspoon coarsely ground
   black pepper + additional
   to season fish
2 (12-ounce) whole rainbow
   trout, cleaned
½ tablespoon butter
4 lemon wedges

**1.** Combine the almonds, cornmeal, salt, and pepper in a food processor or blender and grind to a fine consistency. Transfer to a large, flat plate or a sheet of wax paper. Spray the trout with olive-oil nonstick spray and season with additional salt and pepper, including the cavities of each fish. Roll in the nut mixture to coat all over.

**2.** Melt the butter in a large nonstick skillet over medium heat. Add the trout and brown about 5 minutes on each side. Cover, reduce the heat to low, and cook until the fish is just opaque in the center, 2–3 minutes on each side. Serve with lemon wedges.

Per serving (1 trout): 139 Cal, 8 g Fat, 2 g Sat Fat, 33 mg Chol, 309 mg Sod, 7 g Carb, 1 g Fib, 10 g Prot, 42 mg Calc. *POINTS* value: *3.*

Cornmeal-Almond Trout

# Steamed Sole and Watercress

**MAKES 4 SERVINGS**

Boiling dried shiitake mushrooms softens them, and it also imparts a wonderful depth of flavor to the dressing. You could use cod, halibut, red snapper fillets, or skate wings in place of the sole.

15 small dried shiitake mushrooms, stemmed
1½ cups water
2 tablespoons Scotch whiskey
1 tablespoon canola oil
1 tablespoon red-wine vinegar
¼ teaspoon salt
⅛ teaspoon freshly ground pepper
12 very small red potatoes, halved
4 (4-ounce) sole fillets
1 bunch watercress, stemmed
Snipped chives

1. To make the dressing, combine the mushrooms and water in a small saucepan; bring to a boil and boil until softened, about 6 minutes. Remove the mushrooms. Add the Scotch, oil, and vinegar to the water; bring back to a boil and boil 1 minute longer. Stir in the salt and pepper, cover, and set aside.

2. Place the potatoes in a steamer basket; set in a saucepan over 1 inch of boiling water. Cover tightly and steam until fork-tender, about 10 minutes. Wrap in foil to keep warm. Place a plate that will fit inside the steamer basket and arrange the fish in a single layer on top. Cover tightly and steam until fish turns white and opaque, about 4 minutes.

3. To serve, thinly slice the mushrooms. Divide the watercress among 4 plates; top with a fish fillet, then surround with potatoes and scatter with mushrooms. Drizzle with the dressing and garnish with the chives.

Per serving (1 sole fillet, 3 potatoes, and ¼ of mushrooms): 281 Cal, 5 g Fat, 1 g Sat Fat, 54 mg Chol, 247 mg Sod, 31 g Carb, 3 g Fib, 25 g Prot, 31 mg Calc. *POINTS* value: *5.*

meals in minutes

# Filets Mignons with Shallot-Cognac Sauce

**MAKES 4 SERVINGS**

Filets mignons are steaks cut from the tenderloin, so they are lean, tender, and virtually fuss-free. Searing is a perfect cooking method for them—it's fast and it seals in the juices—since it lessens the chance of the steaks drying out and becoming tough.

1 tablespoon fennel seeds, finely chopped

³/₄ teaspoon coarsely ground black pepper

¹/₂ teaspoon salt

4 (4-ounce) filets mignons, about 1-inch thick, trimmed of all visible fat

¹/₂ teaspoon olive oil

¹/₂ cup dry red wine

¹/₂ cup beef broth

2 shallots, finely chopped

¹/₄ cup cognac

1. On a sheet of wax paper, combine the fennel, pepper, and salt. Coat the steaks on all sides with the mixture.

2. Heat the oil in a medium nonstick skillet over medium-high heat. Add the steaks and cook until browned, about 1 minute on each side. Reduce the heat to medium and cook until an instant-read thermometer inserted into the center of each steak registers 160°F for medium, 145°F for medium-rare, about 4 minutes on each side for medium-rare. Transfer steaks to a serving plate.

3. Add the wine, broth, and shallots to the skillet; bring to a boil, scraping up the browned bits in the bottom of the skillet. Add the cognac; bring to a boil and boil until the pan juices are reduced by half, about 5 minutes. Stir in any juices that have accumulated around the steaks into the shallot sauce. Spoon the sauce over the steaks.

Per serving (1 steak with about 3 tablespoons sauce): 269 Cal, 9 g Fat, 4 g Sat Fat, 70 mg Chol, 485 mg Sod, 8 g Carb, 1 g Fib, 25 g Prot, 43 mg Calc. *POINTS* value: **6.**

*in a jiffy*

To keep the fennel seeds from flying all over as you chop them, drizzle them with just a drop or two of olive oil.

# Orange Beef with Noodles

**MAKES 4 SERVINGS**

Here's a classic Chinese favorite made so simple you'll have dinner on the table in a mere 20 minutes. We use flank steak, but you can also use boneless top round steak.

- 4 ounces rice-stick noodles
- ²/₃ cup orange juice
- 2 tablespoons reduced-sodium soy sauce
- 2 teaspoons sugar
- 1 teaspoon Asian (dark) sesame oil
- 1 teaspoon cornstarch
- ½ teaspoon chili paste
- ½ pound flank steak, trimmed of all visible fat and sliced thin across the grain
- 6 scallions, cut into 2-inch slices
- 2 garlic cloves, minced
- 2 teaspoons minced peeled fresh ginger

1. Prepare the noodles according to package directions; drain and set aside.

2. Combine the orange juice, soy sauce, sugar, oil, cornstarch, and chili paste in a bowl until blended and smooth; set aside.

3. Spray a large nonstick skillet with nonstick spray and set over high heat. Add the steak and cook in batches, until browned, about 5 minutes. Add the scallions, garlic, and ginger. Cook, stirring constantly, until fragrant, about 3 minutes. Stir in the orange juice mixture and cook until the sauce boils and thickens slightly, about 3 minutes. Stir in the noodles; heat through. Serve at once.

Per serving (1¼ cups): 210 Cal, 5 g Fat, 2 g Sat Fat, 32 mg Chol, 342 mg Sod, 26 g Carb, 1 g Fib, 14 g Prot, 34 mg Calc. **POINTS** value: **4.**

When browning meat, make sure it is cooked over high heat in a single layer. If your pan is not big enough to accommodate all the meat at one time, cook it in batches, otherwise the meat will steam instead of brown.

# Spicy Thai Beef Stir-fry

**MAKES 4 SERVINGS**

Full of lively, robust flavors from watercress, lime juice, garlic, fresh ginger, and green curry paste, this spicy stir-fry will excite your taste buds.

³/₄ cup low-sodium
   chicken broth
3 tablespoons fresh
   lime juice
3 tablespoons unsweetened
   coconut milk
2 tablespoons packed dark
   brown sugar
1 tablespoon cornstarch
1 tablespoon fish sauce
   (nam pla)
2 teaspoons Asian (dark)
   sesame oil
¹/₂ teaspoon green
   curry paste
2 teaspoons peanut oil
³/₄ pound flank steak, cut
   across the grain
   diagonally into thin strips
2 garlic cloves, minced
1 teaspoon minced peeled
   fresh ginger
2 yellow bell peppers,
   seeded and cut into
   thin strips
1 bunch watercress, tough
   stems removed (about
   4 cups)
2 cups cooked instant
   brown rice

1. Combine the broth, lime juice, coconut milk, sugar, cornstarch, fish sauce, sesame oil, and curry paste in a bowl; set aside.

2. Heat a large nonstick skillet over high heat until a drop of water sizzles. Pour in 1 teaspoon of the peanut oil and swirl to coat the pan. Add the beef in batches and stir-fry until browned, about 4 minutes. Transfer the beef to a plate. Wipe the skillet clean.

3. Heat the remaining 1 teaspoon peanut oil in the same skillet, then add the garlic and ginger. Stir-fry over medium-high heat until fragrant, about 30 seconds. Add the peppers and cook, stirring constantly, until tender-crisp, about 3 minutes. Add the watercress and cook, stirring, until the watercress begins to wilt, about 3 minutes. Stir in the broth mixture and cook, stirring constantly, until the mixture boils and thickens, about 1 minute. Return the beef to the pan and toss to combine. Serve with the rice.

Per serving (1¹/₂ cups stir-fry and ¹/₂ cup rice): 366 Cal, 14 g Fat, 5 g Sat Fat, 48 mg Chol, 260 mg Sod, 37 g Carb, 3 g Fib, 23 g Prot, 74 mg Calc. **POINTS** value: **8.**

**COOK TO COOK** If you can't find green curry paste in your supermarket or in an Asian grocery, any hot chili paste will do for this recipe.

**Veal Chops with Tomato and Olive Couscous**

# Veal Chops with Tomato and Olive Couscous

**MAKES 4 SERVINGS**

They may be a bit pricey, but when seasoned with a fragrant lemon-parsley rub and cooked just right, veal chops are well worth the expense. Take care not to overcook them because they can dry out easily. This rub also tastes delicious on chicken or pork.

- 2 teaspoons olive oil
- 1 tomato, chopped
- 1 tablespoon minced shallot
- 1 (10-ounce) box plain couscous
- 2 cups low-sodium chicken broth
- 4 oil-cured black olives, pitted and chopped
- 1 tablespoon chopped fresh parsley
- 2 teaspoons dried oregano
- 2 teaspoons grated lemon zest
- 1 garlic clove, minced
- ½ teaspoon salt
- ½ teaspoon freshly ground pepper
- 4 (6-ounce) lean, bone-in veal loin chops, about ½-inch thick, trimmed of all visible fat

**1.** Spray the broiler rack with nonstick spray; preheat the broiler.

**2.** Heat 1 teaspoon of the oil in a medium nonstick saucepan over medium heat. Add the tomato and shallot and cook, stirring, until the tomato is softened, about 4 minutes. Add the couscous, broth, and olives; bring to a boil. Remove from the heat; let stand, covered, 5 minutes. Fluff lightly with a fork.

**3.** Meanwhile, combine the parsley, oregano, lemon zest, garlic, salt, pepper, and the remaining 1 teaspoon oil in a small bowl. Blot the veal chops dry with paper towels. Rub both sides of the veal with the parsley mixture. Broil the veal 5 inches from the heat until an instant-read thermometer inserted into the center of each chop registers 160°F for medium, 145°F for medium-rare, 3–4 minutes on each side for medium-rare. Serve with the couscous mixture.

Per serving (1 veal chop and ¾ cup couscous): 408 Cal, 7 g Fat, 2 g Sat Fat, 62 mg Chol, 417 mg Sod, 58 g Carb, 4 g Fib, 26 g Prot, 54 mg Calc. **POINTS** value: **8.**

*in a jiffy*

# Steak on Garlic Toast with Cherry Tomato Salsa

**MAKES 4 SERVINGS**

Steak sandwiches are always a treat, especially when the bread is slathered with garlic puree and the meat is topped with a fiery salsa. Poaching the garlic is an easy way to mellow its strong taste—and it's a lot quicker and easier than oven-roasting the garlic.

- 6 whole unpeeled garlic cloves
- 3 cups water
- 1 pint grape or cherry tomatoes, halved
- 2 tomatillos, cut into small wedges
- ½ large seedless cucumber, peeled and diced
- ½ red onion, finely chopped
- ¼ cup chopped cilantro
- 1 jalapeño pepper, seeded and minced (wear gloves to prevent irritation)
- 3 tablespoons cider vinegar
- 1 tablespoon extra-virgin olive oil
- ½ teaspoon salt
- 1 (1-pound) boneless beef sirloin steak, trimmed of all visible fat
- 2 teaspoons dried oregano
- 1 teaspoon coarsely ground black pepper
- 4 (1-inch) slices seeded Italian bread, toasted

1. Bring the garlic and the water to a boil in a small saucepan. Reduce the heat and simmer, uncovered, until the garlic is very tender, about 15 minutes. Drain. When the garlic is cool enough to handle, remove the skins; put the garlic into a small bowl and mash. Set aside.

2. Spray the broiler rack with nonstick spray; preheat the broiler.

3. Meanwhile, to prepare the salsa, combine the tomatoes, tomatillos, cucumber, onion, cilantro, jalapeño, vinegar, oil, and salt in a medium bowl. Refrigerate, covered, until ready to serve.

4. Sprinkle the steak with the oregano and black pepper. Broil the steak 5 inches from the heat until an instant-read thermometer inserted into the center of the steak registers 160°F for medium, 145°F for medium-rare, about 5 minutes on each side for medium. Let stand 10 minutes, then thinly slice the steak on an angle across the grain.

5. Spread the toast slices with the garlic spread. Arrange the meat on top of the bread slices. Top with the salsa. Serve at once.

Per serving (1 slice toast, about 4 slices steak, and 1 cup salsa): 291 Cal, 9 g Fat, 2 g Sat Fat, 60 mg Chol, 521 mg Sod, 26 g Carb, 3 g Fib, 27 g Prot, 62 mg Calc. **POINTS** value: **6.**

Tomatillos look like small green tomatoes and are covered with thin papery husks, which need to be removed. They have a firm flesh and a tart, lemony flavor. You can find them in the produce section of most supermarkets.

meals in minutes

# Pork Tenderloin with Pearl Onion Sauce

**MAKES 4 SERVINGS**

Tiny pork tenderloins have liberated pork from the tyranny of lengthy roasting times. We broil the meat in this recipe, but if you prefer, roast the tenderloin in a 425°F oven for 20 minutes, or cook it in a ridged grill pan on the stovetop for 5 minutes on each side. The grill pan produces crusty bands where the ridges sear the mustard into the meat.

½ tablespoon coarse-grain Dijon mustard

1 (1-pound) pork tenderloin, trimmed of all visible fat

½ tablespoon olive oil

1 (6-ounce) bag fresh pearl onions, peeled

1 garlic clove, minced

½ cup low-sodium chicken broth

½ tablespoon balsamic vinegar

1 teaspoon thyme leaves

1 teaspoon packed dark brown sugar

1. Spray the broiler rack with nonstick spray; preheat the broiler. Rub the mustard over the pork to coat; place on the broiler rack. Broil the pork 5 inches from the heat until the pork reaches an internal temperature of 160°F, about 5 minutes on each side. Transfer the pork to a plate, wrap it in foil, and let it stand 10 minutes before thinly slicing.

2. Meanwhile, heat the oil in a medium skillet over medium-high heat. Add the onions and cook, stirring constantly, until they begin to brown, about 4 minutes. Stir in the garlic, then stir in the broth, vinegar, thyme, and brown sugar; bring to a boil and boil until the liquid is reduced by one-third and thickens into a sauce, 3–4 minutes. Spoon over the pork.

Per serving (about 4 slices pork with about ¼ cup sauce): 192 Cal, 6 g Fat, 2 g Sat Fat, 74 mg Chol, 127 mg Sod, 8 g Carb, 1 g Fib, 25 g Prot, 27 mg Calc. *POINTS* value: *4.*

*in a jiffy*

 To peel pearl onions, blanch 2 minutes in boiling water, drain, and rinse briefly under cold running water. Cut off the root ends and slip off the peels. Or use superspeedy thawed frozen pearl onions, which are already peeled.

CHAPTER 5

# a fresh approach

## DELIGHTFUL RECIPES THAT MAKE DELICIOUS USE
## OF THE SEASON'S FRESHEST PRODUCE

# Caramelized Onion Tart

**MAKES 8 SERVINGS**

Onions take on a whole new dimension when paired with spinach pesto and Gruyère cheese in a crisp phyllo crust. Use fresh rather than dried thyme between the layers because the dried variety will become too brittle.

4 **large Vidalia onions,**
**sliced (about 9 cups)**

2 **tablespoons packed light**
**brown sugar**

1 **tablespoon balsamic**
**vinegar**

½ **teaspoon coarsely ground**
**black pepper**

½ **cup spinach, cleaned**

2 **garlic cloves, peeled**

1 **tablespoon vegetable oil**

1 **tablespoon hot water**

4 **sheets phyllo**

3½ **teaspoons chopped**
**thyme leaves**

½ **cup shredded**
**Gruyère cheese**

1. Heat a very large skillet over high heat. Put the onions in the skillet and spray them with olive-oil nonstick spray. Stirring almost constantly, cook until dry and just turning light golden, about 25 minutes. Stir in the brown sugar and vinegar and cook until the onions are dark golden and reduced in volume by two-thirds, about 5 minutes longer. Transfer onions to a bowl and stir in the pepper.

2. Preheat oven to 375°F. Combine the spinach, garlic, oil, and water in a food processor and process until smooth.

3. Fit half of a phyllo sheet snugly into a 7 x 11-inch baking dish, with the other half hanging over the edge. Spray with olive-oil nonstick spray and sprinkle with ½ teaspoon of the thyme. Fold the other half of the phyllo over into the pan, spray it, and sprinkle with another ½ teaspoon thyme. Repeat process with the 3 remaining phyllo sheets to make an 8-layer crust, omitting the sprinkle of thyme on the top. Spread the spinach pesto over the crust, sprinkle with the cheese, and spread onions to cover top to the outer edges. Bake until browned on top, about 20 minutes. Remove from oven, let stand 5 minutes, then cut into 8 squares.

Per serving (1 square): 109 Cal, 5 g Fat, 2 g Sat Fat, 7 mg Chol, 74 mg Sod, 14 g Carb, 1 g Fib, 3 g Prot, 92 mg Calc. **POINTS** value: **2.**

Vidalia onions can vary greatly in size; 4 large or 3 very large onions should yield the 9 cups sliced onion needed for the tart. For an even more substantial entrée, divide the tart into 4 servings; a green salad rounds out the meal.

# Crunchy Zucchini Sticks

**MAKES 6 SERVINGS**

This cornflake coating also works well on other vegetables. Try making crunchy mushroom caps or onion rings, if you like.

1 zucchini, cut into 4 x ¹/₂-inch sticks (about 24)

1 yellow squash, cut into 4 x ¹/₂-inch sticks (about 24)

2 tablespoons reduced-calorie mayonnaise

6 tablespoons cornflake crumbs

1. Preheat the broiler; spray a large baking sheet with nonstick spray. Combine the zucchini, yellow squash, and mayonnaise in a bowl until well coated. Place the cornflake crumbs in a zip-close plastic bag; add the zucchini and yellow squash in batches, shaking the bag to coat both sides.

2. Arrange the vegetables in one layer on the baking sheet. Spray the top of the vegetables with nonstick spray. Broil 7 inches from the heat until the vegetables are tender and golden, about 3 minutes on each side.

Per serving (8 sticks): 40 Cal, 2 g Fat, 0 g Sat Fat, 2 mg Chol, 69 mg Sod, 5 g Carb, 1 g Fib, 1 g Prot, 10 mg Calc. **POINTS** value: **1.**

a fresh approach

# Orange and Red Onion Salad

**MAKES 4 SERVINGS**

Delicate curly endive combines beautifully with sweet oranges, red onion, and fruity niçoise olives. Curly endive is sometimes sold as chicory, but it's actually quite different—a deeper green and not as bitter. It's also sometimes sold as frisée.

1   head curly endive, torn

2   navel oranges, peeled and
      sliced into rounds

16   niçoise olives, pitted
      and halved

½   red onion, thinly sliced

2   teaspoons balsamic
      vinegar

4   teaspoons olive oil

     Freshly ground pepper

**1.** Divide the endive among 4 salad plates. Top with the orange rounds, then scatter with the olives and onion.

**2.** To make the dressing, put the vinegar into a small bowl; while whisking, drizzle in the oil, then whisk in the pepper to taste. Drizzle the dressing over the salads.

Per serving (1 salad): 115 Cal, 6 g Fat, 1 g Sat Fat, 0 mg Chol, 142 mg Sod, 15 g Carb, 6 g Fib, 3 g Prot, 109 mg Calc. ***POINTS*** value: *2.*

**COOK TO COOK**   To pit niçoise (or any) olives, place a few on a cutting board and push down with the side of a chef's knife or a similar kitchen utensil to flatten and split the olives. Then pull the halves of the olives open and remove the pits.

meals in minutes

# Roasted Beet and Asian Pear Salad

**MAKES 6 SERVINGS**

One bunch of beets, which most commonly consists of three beets in varying sizes, usually weighs about a pound. Asian pears, also known as apple pears, are shaped like apples and have golden-brown skins similar to Bosc pears. They are as sweet as a pear but have more of the crunch of an apple.

1 **bunch beets, trimmed**
1 **Asian pear, peeled and chopped**
1 **bunch arugula, cleaned and shredded**
2 **tablespoons tarragon vinegar**
1 **tablespoon fresh lemon juice**
1 **tablespoon olive oil**
¼ **teaspoon salt**
**Freshly ground pepper**

**1.** Preheat the oven to 400°F. Wrap the beets in foil and roast until fork-tender, about 1 hour and 15 minutes. Unwrap the foil and let the beets cool, then peel and chop. In a large bowl combine the beets, half the Asian pear, and the arugula; toss to combine.

**2.** To make the dressing, in a small bowl whisk the vinegar and lemon juice. Drizzle in the oil, whisking constantly, then add the salt and the pepper to taste. Pour over the salad and toss to coat. Serve, scattering the remaining Asian pear over the salads.

Per serving (about ³/₄ cup): 47 Cal, 2 g Fat, 0 g Sat Fat, 0 mg Chol, 128 mg Sod, 7 g Carb, 2 g Fib, 1 g Prot, 8 mg Calc. **POINTS** value: **1.**

**COOK TO COOK** Leave about an inch of stem when you trim the beets, and don't touch the pointy root end until after they're roasted (this helps keep the color in the beets and off your hands, clothes, and counters). Save the tops—a good source of vitamins A and C, and tasty, too. Just cook as you would spinach.

Melon, Prosciutto,
and Fig Salad

# Melon, Prosciutto, and Fig Salad

**MAKES 4 SERVINGS**

This salad derives much of its character from robustly flavored salt-cured prosciutto. Although quite flavorful with dried figs (which are available year-round), it is sublime with fresh figs. They are in season during summer and early fall.

¼ cup + 2 tablespoons honey

2 teaspoons Dijon mustard

2 tablespoons balsamic vinegar

1 bunch watercress, stemmed

1 cantaloupe, seeded, peeled, and thinly sliced

1 honeydew melon, seeded, peeled, and thinly sliced

8 slices prosciutto, quartered and rolled

4 fresh figs, or 4 dried Calimyrna figs, quartered

1. To make the dressing, in a small bowl whisk the honey and mustard; whisk in the vinegar.

2. Divide the watercress among 4 salad plates. Alternate the cantaloupe and honeydew slices in a spoke pattern, intersperse 8 prosciutto rolls between the melon slices on each plate, and scatter the fig quarters over the salad. Drizzle with the dressing.

Per serving (1 salad): 384 Cal, 6 g Fat, 2 g Sat Fat, 45 mg Chol, 911 mg Sod, 67 g Carb, 4 g Fib, 20 g Prot, 64 mg Calc. **POINTS** value: **7.**

**COOK TO COOK** Feel free to be creative as you lay out these salads. For example, you can keep like pieces of fruit together and scatter the prosciutto slices, unrolled, for an elegant presentation.

*a fresh approach*

# Roasted Pepper Salad with Feta Cheese

**MAKES 4 SERVINGS**

Sweet roasted bell peppers are the perfect flavor contrast to tangy feta cheese. This lovely dish has plenty of colors, but for even more contrast use ½ bunch of watercress and 1 small head of Belgian endive, thinly sliced crosswise, instead of only watercress.

1 green bell pepper
1 yellow bell pepper
1 red bell pepper
3 tablespoons balsamic vinegar
1 garlic clove, chopped
½ teaspoon Dijon mustard
⅛ teaspoon salt
Freshly ground pepper
1 bunch watercress, stemmed
¼ cup crumbled feta cheese
12 niçoise olives, pitted and halved
4 teaspoons shredded basil leaves

1. Preheat the broiler. Line a baking sheet with foil; place the bell peppers on the baking sheet. Broil 5 inches from the heat, turning occasionally with tongs, until lightly charred, about 10 minutes. Transfer to a bowl, cover, and let stand for 10 minutes. Peel, seed, and thinly slice the peppers over a bowl to catch the juices.

2. In a medium nonreactive bowl, whisk the vinegar, garlic, and mustard. Add the bell peppers; toss to coat, then sprinkle with the salt and ground pepper to taste. Refrigerate, covered, until chilled, about 30 minutes.

3. Divide the watercress among 4 salad plates; top each with about ½ cup bell peppers and scatter evenly with the cheese, olives, and basil.

Per serving (1 salad): 75 Cal, 3 g Fat, 2 g Sat Fat, 8 mg Chol, 281 mg Sod, 10 g Carb, 3 g Fib, 3 g Prot, 121 mg Calc. **POINTS** value: **1.**

Feel free to use goat cheese instead of the feta, if desired.

*meals in minutes*

# Shrimp, Fennel, and Grapes in Cantaloupe Halves

**MAKES 4 SERVINGS**

Here's an elegant main-dish take on Waldorf salad, offering a delicious mix of succulent shrimp, crunchy fennel, and sweet grapes in a fresh lime dressing. To save time, buy the shrimp precooked at the fish market the day you plan to serve this and omit Step 1.

| | |
|---|---|
| ³/₄ | **pound medium shrimp, peeled and deveined** |
| ¹/₂ | **fennel bulb, trimmed and very thinly sliced, or 1 cup sliced celery** |
| 1 | **cup seedless grapes, halved** |
| 2 | **tablespoons chopped fennel leaves** |
| 2 | **tablespoons reduced-fat mayonnaise** |
| 1 | **tablespoon fresh lime or lemon juice** |
| 2 | **cantaloupes, halved and seeded** |
| 2 | **tablespoons chopped toasted walnuts** |

1. Bring a pot of water to a boil; add the shrimp and simmer until just opaque in the center, 3–4 minutes. Drain in a colander and rinse under cold water to stop the cooking. Dry the shrimp on paper towels.

2. Combine the shrimp, fennel or celery, grapes, fennel leaves, mayonnaise, and lime or lemon juice in a medium bowl. Spoon into the cantaloupe halves, sprinkle with the walnuts, and serve at once.

Per serving (1 cantaloupe half and ³/₄ cup filling): 289 Cal, 7 g Fat, 1 g Sat Fat, 82 mg Chol, 208 mg Sod, 49 g Carb, 5 g Fib, 14 g Prot, 90 mg Calc. *POINTS* value: *6.*

Chopped fennel leaves add flavor to this dish. If you're using celery in place of the fennel, consider adding chopped fresh mint to replace the fennel leaves.

**COOK TO COOK**

a fresh approach

# Chilled Curried Carrot Soup

**MAKES 4 SERVINGS**

This soup is just as good made a day ahead and refrigerated. But beware: The longer the soup sits, the stronger the curry flavor becomes. The addition of fresh ginger accentuates the sweetness of the carrots.

4 **carrots, chunked**
$\frac{1}{2}$ **white onion, roughly chopped**
2 **cups low-sodium chicken broth**
$\frac{1}{2}$ **tablespoon minced peeled fresh ginger**
$\frac{1}{2}$ **teaspoon curry powder**
$\frac{1}{8}$ **teaspoon salt**
$\frac{1}{2}$ **cup light sour cream**
2 **tablespoons fat-free milk**
**Snipped chives**

1. In a medium saucepan, combine the carrots, onion, and broth, then stir in the ginger and curry powder; bring to a boil. Reduce the heat and simmer, covered, until the carrots can be mashed easily, 40–45 minutes.

2. Transfer to a blender or food processor and puree. Transfer to a bowl, add the salt, and refrigerate, tightly covered, at least 2 hours.

3. In a small bowl, whisk the sour cream and milk until smooth. Serve the soup, dolloped with the sour cream mixture and sprinkled with the chives.

Per serving (scant $^{3}/_{4}$ cup soup with $2^{1}/_{2}$ tablespoons sour cream mixture): 93 Cal, 4 g Fat, 3 g Sat Fat, 13 mg Chol, 177 mg Sod, 12 g Carb, 3 g Fib, 5 g Prot, 83 mg Calc. *POINTS* value: *2.*

meals in minutes

# Chilled Tomato Soup with Pesto

**MAKES 4 SERVINGS**

Vine-ripened tomatoes are a must for this soup, so if you need to ripen a few, plan ahead. Ripen tomatoes by putting them with an apple in a paper bag pierced with a few holes. Let stand at room temperature for two to three days.

**Soup:**
- 1 teaspoon olive oil
- 1 white onion, chopped
- 1 garlic clove, minced
- 2 large tomatoes, peeled, seeded, and chopped
- 1 cup vegetable broth

**Pesto:**
- 2 cups loosely packed basil leaves
- 2 tablespoons fresh lemon juice
- ½ tablespoon pine nuts
- 1 garlic clove
- ¼ teaspoon salt
- ⅛ teaspoon freshly ground pepper
- 1 tablespoon olive oil

**1.** Heat the oil in a medium saucepan over medium heat. Add the onion and garlic and cook until softened, about 5 minutes. Stir in the tomatoes and broth; bring to a boil. Reduce the heat and simmer until the tomatoes are falling apart, 15–20 minutes.

**2.** Transfer to a blender or food processor and puree. Transfer the soup to a bowl and refrigerate, tightly covered, at least 2 hours.

**3.** To make the pesto, in a food processor or blender puree the basil, lemon juice, pine nuts, garlic, salt, and pepper. With the machine running, drizzle in the oil; puree. Serve the soup, topped with a dollop of the pesto.

Per serving (¾ cup soup with about 1 tablespoon pesto): 96 Cal, 6 g Fat, 1 g Sat Fat, 0 mg Chol, 406 mg Sod, 11 g Carb, 3 g Fib, 3 g Prot, 79 mg Calc. **POINTS** value: **2.**

**COOK TO COOK**

This low-fat pesto is very versatile. Use it to top a piece of broiled white fish or to accent a rice salad. Or combine it with chopped tomatoes on toasted bread rounds for a tasty Italian-style appetizer.

# Chilly Dilly Cucumber Soup

**MAKES 4 SERVINGS**

For this recipe, look for a long, thin hothouse (or English) cucumber, which is bred to be seedless. They usually come wrapped in plastic, which seals in the moisture and helps to prolong freshness. (It also means the cucumber doesn't need to be waxed.)

1 seedless cucumber, peeled and chunked
1½ cups vegetable broth
8 scallions, chunked (white and light green parts only)
¼ cup chopped fresh dill
¼ cup light sour cream
Snipped dill

**1.** In a food processor or blender puree the cucumber, broth, scallions, and chopped dill. Transfer to a bowl and refrigerate, tightly covered, at least 2 hours.

**2.** Stir in the sour cream until well blended. Serve, sprinkled with the dill.

Per serving (1½ cups): 66 Cal, 3 g Fat, 1 g Sat Fat, 5 mg Chol, 402 mg Sod, 15 g Carb, 3 g Fib, 6 g Prot, 192 mg Calc. **POINTS** value: **1.**

**COOK TO COOK**

For an extra bit of zip, stir a pinch of cayenne or crushed red pepper into the soup before refrigerating.

meals in minutes

# Cream of Cauliflower Soup

**MAKES 6 SERVINGS**

If you love the taste of cauliflower but don't know how to use it, this is a great recipe to try. When selecting, cauliflower should have creamy white, compact florets with firmly attached bright green leaves.

- 2 teaspoons olive oil
- 1 white onion, chopped
- 1 head cauliflower, broken into florets
- 3 cups low-sodium chicken broth
- ³/₄ cup evaporated fat-free milk
- ¹/₄ teaspoon freshly grated nutmeg
- ¹/₈ teaspoon ground white pepper
- ¹/₄ teaspoon salt
- 6 chervil or flat-leaf parsley leaves

**1.** Heat the oil in a large nonstick saucepan or Dutch oven over medium-high heat. Add the onion and cook, stirring constantly, until tender, about 5 minutes. Add the cauliflower and cook, stirring, until heated through, about 5 minutes. Add the broth; bring to a boil. Reduce the heat to medium-low and simmer, covered, until the vegetables can be easily mashed, about 10 minutes.

**2.** Transfer to a blender or food processor and puree. Pour the puree back into the saucepan. Over low heat stir in the evaporated milk, nutmeg, pepper, and salt; heat to serving temperature, about 1 minute. Serve, garnished with a chervil or parsley leaf.

Per serving (1 cup): 83 Cal, 3 g Fat, 1 g Sat Fat, 5 mg Chol, 265 mg Sod, 10 g Carb, 3 g Fib, 6 g Prot, 35 mg Calc. *POINTS* value: *1.*

a fresh approach

# Minted Pea Soup

**MAKES 4 SERVINGS**

Fresh green peas, which are in season from June through August, are noted for their subtle sweetness. The appliance you use to puree the soup will determine its texture. For a smoother soup, use the blender; a food processor will yield a slightly coarser puree.

**4 cups fresh or frozen peas**
**2 cups low-sodium chicken broth**
**1/8 teaspoon ground white pepper**
**1/4 teaspoon salt**
**1/4 cup chopped fresh mint**
**1/4 cup light sour cream**
**Mint sprigs**

1. In a large saucepan, combine the peas and broth; bring to a boil. Reduce the heat and simmer, covered, until the peas are tender but still bright green, about 5 minutes.
2. Transfer to a blender or food processor and puree. Transfer to a bowl, stir in the white pepper and salt, and refrigerate, tightly covered, at least 2 hours.
3. Stir in the chopped mint. Serve, garnished with the sour cream and a sprig of mint.

Per serving (generous 1 cup with 1 tablespoon sour cream): 148 Cal, 3 g Fat, 2 g Sat Fat, 8 mg Chol, 371 mg Sod, 22 g Carb, 7 g Fib, 10 g Prot, 89 mg Calc. *POINTS* value: *2.*

For 4 cups fresh peas, you'll need 4 pounds of peas in the pod.

meals in minutes

# Garlicky Potato Salad

**MAKES 4 SERVINGS**

Don't let the amount of garlic in this recipe throw you; roasting the cloves mellows and sweetens their flavor. Use Yukon Gold or Yellow Finn potatoes instead of red if a buttery taste is what you're after.

8 garlic cloves, unpeeled
8 small red potatoes, cut into 8 pieces each
$1/2$ cup reduced-fat mayonnaise
2 scallions, thinly sliced
1 teaspoon sweet paprika
1 teaspoon snipped chives
$1/2$ teaspoon salt
$1/8$ teaspoon freshly ground pepper
2 cups mesclun

1. Preheat the oven to 350°F. Wrap the garlic cloves in foil and bake until softened, about 45 minutes. Let cool 10 minutes, then remove foil and peel.

2. Meanwhile, put the potatoes in a steamer basket; set in a saucepan over 1 inch of boiling water. Cover tightly and steam the potatoes until fork-tender, about 6 minutes.

3. In a bowl, mix the mayonnaise, scallions, paprika, chives, salt, and pepper; press in the garlic with a garlic press. Fold in the potatoes. Refrigerate, covered, until chilled, at least 30 minutes.

4. To serve, divide the mesclun among 4 plates and top with the potato salad.

Per serving (about $1/2$ cup each potato salad and mesclun): 239 Cal, 6 g Fat, 1 g Sat Fat, 7 mg Chol, 463 mg Sod, 43 g Carb, 4 g Fib, 5 g Prot, 61 mg Calc. *POINTS* value: *4.*

**COOK TO COOK** This salad will keep refrigerated for up to three days. If you have the foresight to make it ahead, you're in for a bonus: Its flavor just gets more robust. For a spicier salad, use $1/2$ teaspoon hot paprika in lieu of the sweet.

# Roasted Ratatouille Lasagna

**MAKES 6 SERVINGS**

If you think of vegetarian lasagna as bland, wait till you try this version. Roasting intensifies the flavors and imparts an intriguing smoky nuance to vegetables. Using no-boil noodles saves at least 30 minutes of prep time. Spray the foil lightly with nonstick spray before covering the lasagna to help keep the cheese from sticking to it.

1 medium (1-pound) eggplant, chunked
2 medium zucchini, chunked
4 plum tomatoes, halved
1 yellow bell pepper, seeded and quartered
1 white onion, chunked
1 garlic bulb
1 cup part-skim ricotta cheese
2 tablespoons grated Parmesan cheese
2 tablespoons chopped fresh basil
1 egg white
¼ teaspoon freshly ground pepper
8 no-boil lasagna noodles
1 cup shredded part-skim mozzarella cheese

**1.** Preheat the oven to 375°F. Spray a baking sheet with nonstick spray. Scatter the eggplant, zucchini, tomatoes, bell pepper, and onion on the baking sheet; spray with nonstick spray. Wrap the garlic in foil. Roast the vegetables until well browned, about 45 minutes, tossing every 15 minutes. Roast the garlic at the same time until softened, about 45 minutes. Cool the vegetables, then peel the bell pepper, tomatoes, and garlic.

**2.** In a food processor puree the tomatoes and garlic. Finely chop the bell pepper, eggplant, zucchini, and onion. In a large bowl, combine all the vegetables.

**3.** In a small bowl mix the ricotta, Parmesan, basil, egg white, and ground pepper. Spray a 7 x 11-inch baking dish with nonstick spray. Spread ¼ cup of the vegetable mixture over the bottom of the baking dish; top with 2 noodles. Spread an additional 1½ cups of the vegetable mixture over the noodles; top with 2 more noodles. Spread with all the ricotta mixture; top with 2 more noodles. Spread with an additional 1 cup of the vegetable mixture, top with the last 2 noodles and the remaining vegetable mixture; sprinkle with the mozzarella. Cover with foil and bake 30 minutes. Remove the foil and bake until the cheese is melted and browned, about 5 minutes longer.

Per serving (⅙ of lasagna): 268 Cal, 8 g Fat, 4 g Sat Fat, 25 mg Chol, 196 mg Sod, 34 g Carb, 4 g Fib, 16 g Prot, 291 mg Calc. *POINTS* value: *5.*

*meals in minutes*

Roasted
Ratatouille
Lasagna

# Baked Eggplant with Tomato and Basil

**MAKES 6 SERVINGS**

Fans of eggplant parmigiana are going to love this healthful rendition. Broiling the eggplant achieves a similar taste and texture to the usual, more cumbersome process of dipping the slices into a batter, breading, and then frying them. It also eliminates the need to salt the eggplant to remove the bitterness.

2 medium (1 pound each) eggplants, cut into ½-inch rounds
3 cups marinara sauce
24 large basil leaves
1¼ cups shredded part-skim mozzarella cheese

**1.** Preheat the broiler. Put the eggplant in a single layer on a baking sheet and spray with nonstick spray. Broil until well browned, about 4 minutes. Turn the rounds over, spray again, and broil until well browned on the other side, about 4 minutes longer. Remove from the oven and reduce the temperature to 375°F.

**2.** Spread 1 cup of marinara sauce in a shallow 11 x 14-inch baking dish. Add the eggplant rounds, overlapping slightly. Top with the remaining 2 cups sauce, then the basil leaves; sprinkle with the cheese. Bake until the sauce is heated through and the cheese has begun to brown, about 20 minutes. Let stand about 10 minutes before cutting.

Per serving (¹⁄₆ of eggplant): 185 Cal, 8 g Fat, 3 g Sat Fat, 14 mg Chol, 901 mg Sod, 23 g Carb, 4 g Fib, 9 g Prot, 188 mg Calc. **POINTS** value: **4.**

To serve this as an appetizer, slice the eggplant lengthwise, top each slice with basil and cheese, roll up, and secure with toothpicks before baking in the marinara sauce.

meals in minutes

# Caponata Pita

Caponata, a Sicilian specialty composed of eggplant, onions, tomatoes, anchovies, olives, and vinegar, is typically a long-cooked dish in which copious amounts of oil are used. In this quick and light version, roasted eggplant is tossed with raw accompaniments, yielding a crisper caponata and allowing for the minimal use of oil.

| | |
|---|---|
| 1 | (12-ounce) eggplant, cut into $1/2$-inch cubes |
| $1/2$ | tablespoon coarse salt |
| $1/4$ | cup arugula leaves |
| 1 | tablespoon anchovy paste |
| 1 | tablespoon fresh lemon juice |
| 1 | tablespoon tarragon vinegar |
| 1 | teaspoon olive oil |
| 1 | teaspoon dried basil |
| 1 | teaspoon fennel seeds |
| 1 | large tomato, seeded and chopped |
| 1 | small Vidalia onion, chopped |
| 6 | green olives, pitted and coarsely chopped |
| 8 | kalamata olives, pitted and coarsely chopped |
| $1^1/2$ | cups mesclun |
| 3 | (6-inch) pitas, halved crosswise |

**1.** Toss the eggplant with the salt, and let stand 15 minutes. Preheat the oven to 350°F. Spray a baking sheet with nonstick spray. Place the eggplant on the tray in a single layer and bake 20 minutes. Toss the eggplant cubes and bake 10 minutes longer.

**2.** Meanwhile, to make the dressing, puree the arugula, anchovy paste, lemon juice, vinegar, oil, basil, and fennel seeds in a food processor or blender.

**3.** Combine the eggplant, tomato, onion, and olives in a bowl. Add the dressing and toss to coat. Stuff $1/4$ cup of the mesclun into each pita half and fill with about $1/3$ cup of the eggplant mixture.

Per serving ($1/2$ stuffed pita): 142 Cal, 3 g Fat, 0 g Sat Fat, 1 mg Chol, 1,057 mg Sod, 25 g Carb, 3 g Fib, 4 g Prot, 65 mg Calc. **POINTS** value: **2.**

**COOK TO COOK**

When you're pureeing a small amount of food (such as a dressing, as in this recipe), use a mini food processor rather than a standard-size food processor or blender. The food will puree faster in the smaller work bowl, and you'll have to scrape down the sides less frequently.

*a fresh approach*

# Mixed Vegetable Monte Cristo

**MAKES 4 SERVINGS**

Monte Cristo is a classic chicken and Swiss cheese sandwich that's dipped in beaten egg and grilled in butter until golden brown. This meatless version, filled with a savory blend of four vegetables and fresh mozzarella, is baked instead, achieving the same crispness without an overload of fat. Be sure to remove the stems and ribs from the chard leaves. One large portobello mushroom, chopped, can replace the white mushrooms.

½ tablespoon olive oil

6 oil-packed sun-dried tomatoes, drained, patted dry with paper towels, and sliced

1 yellow onion, sliced

1 cup sliced white mushrooms

1 bunch red chard, trimmed and torn

½ teaspoon salt

¼ teaspoon coarsely ground black pepper

2 teaspoons Dijon mustard

8 (½-inch) slices Italian bread

2 ounces fresh mozzarella cheese, very thinly sliced

½ cup fat-free egg substitute

¼ cup fat-free milk

1 tablespoon grated Parmesan cheese

**1.** Put a heavy-gauge nonstick baking sheet in the oven and preheat the oven to 400°F. Heat the oil in a nonstick skillet over high heat. Add the sun-dried tomatoes and onion and cook 2 minutes. Add the mushrooms and cook 5 minutes longer. Add the chard, cover, and cook until wilted, about 2 minutes. Uncover and cook until all the liquid is absorbed, about 1 minute. Stir in the salt and pepper.

**2.** Spread ½ teaspoon of the mustard on each of 4 slices of the bread. Place them on a large plate and spread ¼ cup of the vegetable mixture on each slice. Divide the mozzarella among the sandwiches and top each with a remaining slice of bread.

**3.** Mix together the egg substitute, milk, and Parmesan in a small bowl. Pour over the sandwiches and let stand about 10 minutes. Spray the baking sheet with nonstick spray. Transfer the sandwiches to the baking sheet and bake until well browned and firm to the touch, about 8 minutes on each side.

Per serving (1 sandwich): 291 Cal, 8 g Fat, 3 g Sat Fat, 13 mg Chol, 1,081 mg Sod, 41 g Carb, 4 g Fib, 15 g Prot, 251 mg Calc.
***POINTS*** value: *6.*

meals in minutes

# Pancetta, Fava Bean, and Artichoke Farrotto

**MAKES 4 SERVINGS**

Farro is a grain that's common in Italy, where it is sometimes prepared like risotto. It's like very firm barley, though it is actually a variety of wheat. We call for barley because it's so much more readily available, but if you find farro (try a natural-foods store), soak it overnight in water, then increase the cooking time to about 45 minutes.

1 ounce pancetta, sliced
1 large shallot, chopped
1 garlic clove, chopped
³/₄ cup pearl barley or farro
2³/₄ cups chicken broth
¹/₄ cup dry white wine
1 pound fava beans, shelled, blanched, and peeled
1 (14-ounce) can artichoke hearts, rinsed, drained, and sliced
2 tablespoons sliced fresh basil
¹/₄ cup grated Parmesan cheese
1 teaspoon butter

1. Heat a medium saucepan over medium-high heat. Add the pancetta and cook until lightly browned. Add the shallot and garlic and cook until the shallot turns translucent, about 1 minute. Stir in the barley or farro, then the broth and wine. Bring to a boil, then cover, reduce the heat to medium, and cook 35 minutes.

2. Stir in the fava beans, artichoke hearts, and basil. Cover and continue to cook until all of the liquid is absorbed, about 5 minutes longer. Stir in the Parmesan and butter.

Per serving (about 1¹/₄ cups): 305 Cal, 10 g Fat, 4 g Sat Fat, 16 mg Chol, 934 mg Sod, 42 g Carb, 13 g Fib, 11 g Prot, 146 mg Calc. *POINTS* value: *6.*

**COOK TO COOK** To prepare fava beans, remove them from their pods and peel (unless the beans are very young and tender), a task made much easier by first blanching the beans. Bring a medium saucepan of water to a boil; add a little salt and the fava beans. Cook for 30 seconds, drain, and rinse briefly under cold water.

Winter
Vegetable
Pasta

# Winter Vegetable Pasta

**MAKES 4 SERVINGS**

Use dried capellini for this recipe; angel-hair pasta is a bit too thin to match with these chunky vegetables. The simple cumin- and coriander-infused broth that serves as a sauce complements the sweetness of the squash and corn.

1 **parsnip, cut into matchstick-size pieces**

1⅓ **cups butternut squash, cut into matchstick-size pieces**

2 **teaspoons olive oil**

1 **cup fresh or thawed frozen corn kernels**

1 **small leek, cleaned and sliced**

¾ **cup chicken broth**

¾ **teaspoon ground cumin**

½ **teaspoon ground coriander**

½ **pound capellini**

1½ **cups sugar snap peas**

2 **teaspoons grated Parmesan cheese**

1. Put a heavy-gauge baking sheet into the oven and preheat oven to 400°F. Combine the parsnip and squash in a bowl and toss with 1½ teaspoons of the oil. In a second bowl, toss the corn in the remaining ½ teaspoon of oil. Put the parsnip and squash mixture on the baking sheet and roast 5 minutes. Add the corn and roast for another 5 minutes. Stir and roast until all of the vegetables are lightly browned, about 5 minutes longer. Transfer the vegetables to a large bowl.

2. Spray a medium nonstick skillet with nonstick spray and set over high heat. Add the leek and cook until lightly browned, 4–5 minutes. Stir in the broth, cumin, and coriander. Cook 3 minutes, then remove from the heat.

3. Bring a large pot of water to a boil. Add the capellini and cook 2 minutes, then add the sugar snap peas and cook 30 seconds longer. Drain and add the pasta and sugar snap peas to the vegetables in the bowl. Add the leek sauce and toss to coat. Sprinkle with the Parmesan.

Per serving (generous 1½ cups): 318 Cal, 5 g Fat, 1 g Sat Fat, 2 mg Chol, 417 mg Sod, 60 g Carb, 7 g Fib, 12 g Prot, 106 mg Calc. *POINTS* value: *6.*

a fresh approach

# Wild Mushroom Risotto with Chicken

**MAKES 4 SERVINGS**

Go to any large supermarket these days and you'll find a wide variety of exotic mushrooms. That's good news for dishes like this one, which features a mix of white, shiitake, and oyster mushrooms.

1 teaspoon olive oil
1½ cups sliced white mushrooms
1½ cups sliced shiitake mushrooms
½ cup stemmed oyster mushrooms
3½ cups low-sodium chicken broth
1 cup Arborio rice
2 tablespoons grated Parmesan cheese
⅛ teaspoon freshly ground pepper
½ pound skinless boneless chicken breast

1. Heat oil in a large nonstick skillet over medium-high heat. Add all the mushrooms and cook until they have given off their moisture and are soft, about 6 minutes.

2. Meanwhile, in a medium saucepan, bring the broth to a boil. Reduce the heat and simmer. Spray a broiler rack with nonstick spray; preheat the broiler.

3. Heat a medium nonstick saucepan over medium-high heat. Add the rice and cook, stirring, until lightly toasted. Reduce the heat to medium. Add 1 cup of the broth; cook, stirring until the broth is absorbed. Stir in the mushrooms. Continue adding broth, ½ cup at a time, stirring until the broth is absorbed before adding more, until the rice is tender. The total cooking time should be 25–30 minutes. Stir in the cheese and the pepper.

4. Meanwhile, broil the chicken 5 inches from the heat until cooked through and browned, about 2 minutes on each side. Cut into strips. Serve the risotto, topping each portion with strips of chicken.

Per serving (about 1 cup risotto with about 6 strips chicken): 304 Cal, 5 g Fat, 2 g Sat Fat, 40 mg Chol, 194 mg Sod, 44 g Carb, 3 g Fib, 22 g Prot, 72 mg Calc. *POINTS* value: *6.*

Oyster mushrooms do not have to be chopped. When the thick, woody stem is cut off, the mushroom separates into small sections. If you prefer, you can omit the oyster mushrooms and use two cups of shiitakes.

# Venison Steaks with Blackberry Sauce

**MAKES 4 SERVINGS**

Venison is available at specialty butchers and some supermarkets, but you may need to order it in advance. The blackberry sauce can be prepared with frozen berries if fresh are not in season. The sauce is also delicious with chicken breasts or, if you're really adventurous, ostrich steaks.

1 teaspoon extra-virgin olive oil
1 fennel bulb, thinly sliced
1 small head radicchio, shredded
1 pint fresh blackberries
½ cup vegetable broth
2 sprigs thyme
1 tablespoon cornstarch
¼ cup orange juice
2 (6-ounce) venison steaks

1. Heat oil in a large nonstick skillet over medium-low heat. Add the fennel and radicchio and cook, stirring occasionally, until very soft, about 30 minutes. Meanwhile, spray a broiler rack with nonstick spray; preheat the broiler or grill.

2. Reserve 8–12 blackberries; combine the remainder in a small saucepan with the broth and thyme; bring to a boil, then cook until the berries are easily mashed, about 2 minutes. Transfer to a fine-mesh sieve set over a bowl; press the berries with the back of a spoon, taking care to scrape the residue from the outside of the sieve into the bowl. Return the puree to the saucepan.

3. In a small bowl, dissolve the cornstarch in the orange juice. Add to the puree. Cook over medium heat, stirring constantly, until the mixture thickens, bubbles, and turns translucent, about 2 minutes.

4. Broil or grill the steaks 5 inches from the heat until an instant-read thermometer inserted into the center of each steak registers 160°F for medium, 145°F for medium-rare, about 1½ minutes on each side for medium-rare. Slice into thin strips.

5. To serve, divide the vegetables among 4 plates; fan the steak slices on top, then drizzle with the sauce. Garnish with the reserved berries.

Per serving (⅓ cup vegetables, ½ of 1 steak, ⅓ cup sauce, and 2–3 berries): 217 Cal, 5 g Fat, 2 g Sat Fat, 48 mg Chol, 225 mg Sod, 22 g Carb, 7 g Fib, 23 g Prot, 78 mg Calc. *POINTS* value: **4.**

a fresh approach

# such a comfort

## DISHES THAT INSPIRE YOU TO SAY, "AH, HOME," WHEN YOU TAKE THE FIRST BITE

Herb Cheese–Stuffed Shells

# Herb Cheese–Stuffed Shells

**MAKES 4 SERVINGS**

Boursin cheese is triple-cream, which means it has a marvelously rich, creamy texture—not surprising, since it has at least 75 percent milk fat. These ample shells are stuffed with a homemade low-fat version of Boursin. The cheese is often flavored with herbs; our recipe calls for Italian seasoning for convenience, but by all means substitute herbes de Provence if you have any on hand. The yellow tomatoes used in the sauce are sweeter than red tomatoes and lend a pretty hue.

16 jumbo pasta shells
1 (15-ounce) container fat-free ricotta cheese
½ cup shredded mozzarella cheese
2 tablespoons low-fat buttermilk
1 large egg, beaten
¼ cup chopped yellow onion
2 teaspoons Italian seasoning
½ teaspoon salt
¼ teaspoon coarsely ground black pepper
3 garlic cloves, peeled
1 medium white onion, sliced
6 yellow tomatoes, chopped
1 carrot, grated
½ cup dry white wine
1 tablespoon chopped fresh basil
Pinch crushed red pepper

**1.** Cook shells according to package directions. Drain and rinse briefly under cold running water to stop the cooking.

**2.** Preheat the oven to 350°F. Spray a 9 x 13-inch baking dish with nonstick spray. Mix together the ricotta, mozzarella, buttermilk, egg, onion, Italian seasoning, salt, and pepper; press in the garlic with a garlic press. Stuff 2 tablespoons of the mixture into each shell and set in the baking dish.

**3.** Spray a nonstick skillet with nonstick spray and set over medium heat. Add the white onion and cook until golden brown, 10–12 minutes. Add the tomatoes, carrot, wine, basil, and crushed red pepper. Cook, stirring occasionally, until mixture becomes a thick sauce, 12–15 minutes. Pour over the shells and spread evenly. Cover with foil and bake until hot and bubbling, about 30 minutes.

Per serving (4 stuffed shells with ¼ of sauce): 402 Cal, 9 g Fat, 5 g Sat Fat, 112 mg Chol, 664 mg Sod, 49 g Carb, 5 g Fib, 32 g Prot, 569 mg Calc. *POINTS* value: *8.*

such a comfort

# French Onion and Roasted Garlic Soup

**MAKES 4 SERVINGS**

You'll need about 2 pounds of onions for this recipe, but it doesn't matter whether you choose the common yellow, red, sweet, or white onion, or a mix of varieties. If you love the flavor of freshly roasted garlic but not the time involved, look for vacuum-packed whole roasted garlic cloves, which can be found refrigerated with fresh pastas, or minced roasted garlic in jars, which can be found in the produce section.

1 garlic bulb
1 tablespoon olive oil
4–5 yellow onions,
      thinly sliced
¼ cup dry Marsala
4 cups fat-free beef broth
4 tablespoons shredded
      Gruyère cheese

1. Preheat the oven to 350°F. Wrap the garlic bulb in foil and bake until softened, about 45 minutes; let cool 10 minutes, then remove the foil. Cut the top off the garlic bulb and separate the cloves.

2. Heat the oil a large saucepan over medium heat. Add the onions and cook, stirring occasionally, until they turn golden and begin to caramelize, about 45 minutes. Squeeze the garlic pulp into the onions, discarding the peels; stir until fragrant, about 30 seconds. Stir in the Marsala and broth; bring to a boil. Reduce the heat and simmer gently, covered, 15 minutes. Serve, topped with the cheese.

Per serving (1⅓ cups soup and 1 tablespoon cheese): 152 Cal, 6 g Fat, 2 g Sat Fat, 7 mg Chol, 102 mg Sod, 14 g Carb, 2 g Fib, 9 g Prot, 98 mg Calc. *POINTS* value: *3.*

If you have ovenproof soup crocks, replace the shredded cheese with thin slices. Ladle the soup into the crocks, top each with a slice of Gruyère, and broil until the cheese is lightly browned and beginning to melt.

meals in minutes

# Leek and Potato Soup

**MAKES 4 SERVINGS**

You won't miss the cream usually found in this silky-smooth soup. Like spinach, leeks grow in sandy soil, so it's important to clean them thoroughly. Don't discard the green tops: Save them to toss into stocks for a subtle flavor. This soup can also be refrigerated and served chilled.

3½ cups low-sodium chicken broth

4 leeks, trimmed to white and light-green parts, cleaned, and thinly sliced

1 large red potato, peeled and cubed

Snipped fresh chives

**1.** In a medium saucepan, combine the broth, leeks, and potato; bring to a boil. Reduce heat and simmer, covered, until the vegetables are fork-tender, about 45 minutes.

**2.** Transfer to a blender or food processor and puree (in batches if necessary). Pour the puree back into the saucepan and heat to serving temperature, 1–2 minutes. Serve, garnished with the chives.

Per serving (1⅓ cups): 64 Cal, 2 g Fat, 1 g Sat Fat, 4 mg Chol, 101 mg Sod, 11 g Carb, 1 g Fib, 4 g Prot, 26 mg Calc. *POINTS* value: *1.*

such a comfort

 To trim a leek, cut off the dark green leaves and halve lengthwise. Fan the leaves open under cold running water to rinse off any residual dirt. Lay flat on a board, trim the root ends, and slice as desired.

# Chicken with Currant–Pine Nut Risotto

**MAKES 4 SERVINGS**

Sweet currants and crunchy pine nuts give a welcome contrast of flavors and textures to this creamy risotto—a perfect accompaniment to the simple lemon chicken. Complete the meal with a mesclun salad.

3 cups low-sodium chicken broth
1 tablespoon olive oil
1 onion, finely chopped
1¼ cups Arborio rice
½ cup dry white wine
¼ cup currants
¼ cup pine nuts
¼ cup chopped flat-leaf parsley
¼ teaspoon freshly ground pepper
4 (¼-pound) skinless boneless chicken breasts
1 teaspoon grated lemon zest
½ teaspoon salt
4 lemon wedges

1. To prepare the risotto, bring the broth to a boil in a medium saucepan. Reduce the heat and keep at a simmer.

2. Heat the oil in a large nonstick saucepan over medium heat. Add the onion and cook, stirring frequently, until softened, 3–5 minutes. Add the rice and cook until lightly toasted, 2–3 minutes.

3. Add the wine and ½ cup of the broth to the onion-rice mixture. Cook, stirring until the liquid is absorbed. Continue to add broth, ½ cup at a time, stirring until it is absorbed before adding more, until the rice is just tender and the mixture is creamy. (The cooking time from the first addition of broth should be 20–24 minutes.) Stir in the currants, pine nuts, parsley, and pepper.

4. Sprinkle the chicken with the lemon zest and salt. Spray a nonstick skillet with nonstick spray and set over medium heat. Add the chicken and cook until lightly browned and just cooked through, about 5 minutes on each side. Transfer to a plate, let rest 5 minutes, then thinly slice on the diagonal. Serve with the risotto and lemon wedges.

Per serving (1 chicken breast and 1 cup risotto): 486 Cal, 12 g Fat, 2 g Sat Fat, 62 mg Chol, 403 mg Sod, 60 g Carb, 3 g Fib, 33 g Prot, 57 mg Calc. *POINTS* value: *10.*

meals in minutes

Chicken with
Currant–Pine Nut Risotto

# Lemon-Oregano Chicken

**MAKES 6 SERVINGS**

In this version of the Greek classic, the seasoning is stuffed beneath the skin, so it's not necessary to eat the fatty skin to enjoy the full flavor. If you don't have a food processor, you can mix the herb paste by hand with the back of a spoon.

2 tablespoons oregano leaves

1 garlic clove, peeled

1 tablespoon olive oil

³/₄ teaspoon grated lemon zest

3 tablespoons fresh lemon juice

1 (4-pound) chicken

½ tablespoon arrowroot

1³/₄ cups chicken broth

⅛ teaspoon ground white pepper

1. Preheat the oven to 400°F. Combine the oregano, garlic, oil, lemon zest, and 1 tablespoon of the lemon juice in a food processor; process to a smooth paste. Gently lift the skin away from the chicken and push the paste under the skin, spreading to cover the entire breast. Tuck the wings behind the chicken, and place it on a rack in a roasting pan, breast-side up. Roast until an instant-read thermometer inserted into the thigh registers 180°F, about 1¼–1½ hours.

2. Transfer the chicken to a cutting board and let it stand while you make the sauce. Dissolve the arrowroot in the remaining 2 tablespoons of lemon juice. Bring the broth to a boil in a small saucepan. Boil 5 minutes, remove from the heat, and stir in the dissolved arrowroot. Return the pan to the heat and boil until the sauce is thick and clear, about 2 minutes. Stir in the white pepper. Carve the chicken, removing the skin before eating. Serve with the sauce on the side.

Per serving (¹/₆ chicken with about ¹/₄ cup sauce): 204 Cal, 7 g Fat, 2 g Sat Fat, 87 mg Chol, 366 mg Sod, 2 g Carb, 0 g Fib, 32 g Prot, 23 mg Calc. **POINTS** value: **5.**

Don't truss the chicken or even tie the legs together; leaving the cavity open allows greater heat circulation, so the bird cooks faster.

meals in minutes

# Roast Chicken with Chestnut-Cherry Stuffing

**MAKES 6 SERVINGS**

Roasted chestnuts, dried cherries, and kale make a robust stuffing for this classic Sunday roast. You should get about one cup shelled chestnuts from ½ pound fresh chestnuts. To save time, substitute half of a 15-ounce jar of peeled roasted chestnuts, chopped, or 1 (10-ounce) can of water-packed whole chestnuts, drained and chopped.

1 (3½-pound) roasting chicken
½ teaspoon salt
1 lemon, quartered
3 large garlic cloves, halved
4 sprigs rosemary, or 1 teaspoon dried
2 teaspoons butter
1 red onion, chopped
¾ cup low-sodium chicken broth
3 cups herb-seasoned stuffing mix
½ pound fresh chestnuts, roasted and chopped
½ (10-ounce) package frozen chopped kale, thawed and drained
½ cup chopped dried cherries (or cranberries)
2 tablespoons cognac
Rosemary sprigs (optional)

1. Preheat the oven to 400°F. Spray the rack of a roasting pan with nonstick spray and place the rack in the pan. Spray an 8-inch-square baking dish with nonstick spray.
2. Lightly spray the outside of the chicken with nonstick spray and sprinkle with the salt. Place the lemon, garlic, and rosemary inside the cavity of the chicken. Tuck the wings behind the chicken, then place the chicken, breast-side up, on the rack in the roasting pan.
3. Roast the chicken 25 minutes. Reduce the oven temperature to 350°F and roast until the skin is lightly browned and an instant-read thermometer inserted into the thigh registers 180°F, about 50 minutes longer.
4. Meanwhile, melt the butter in a large nonstick saucepan over medium heat. Add the onion and cook, stirring frequently, until softened, 3–5 minutes. Add the broth, stuffing mix, chestnuts, kale, cherries, and cognac; cook, stirring frequently, until hot, 2–3 minutes. Spoon into baking dish. Cover with foil and bake alongside the chicken 20 minutes; uncover and bake until heated through and top is lightly browned, about 10 minutes longer.
5. Let the chicken stand 10 minutes before carving. Remove and discard the lemon, garlic, and rosemary. Remove and discard the skin, then carve. Serve with the stuffing. Garnish with the rosemary sprigs (if using).

Per serving (⅙ chicken and scant 1 cup stuffing): 410 Cal, 9 g Fat, 3 g Sat Fat, 80 mg Chol, 680 mg Sod, 47 g Carb, 5 g Fib, 33 g Prot, 102 mg Calc. *POINTS* value: *8.*

such a comfort

Chicken and
Artichoke Vesuvio

# Chicken and Artichoke Vesuvio

**MAKES 4 SERVINGS**

This old-time Chicago dish is usually loaded with oil, but our healthy rendition replaces most of it with white wine and lemon juice. The recipe retains lots of garlic and rosemary, the principal flavors of Vesuvio preparations. The artichokes, a novel addition, roast beautifully, emerging with crisp exteriors and buttery insides.

¼ cup fresh lemon juice (from 1–2 medium lemons)

¼ cup dry white wine

6 garlic cloves, minced

1 tablespoon olive oil

2 tablespoons chopped fresh rosemary

4 (6-ounce) skinless boneless chicken breasts

4 medium baking potatoes, each cut lengthwise into 8 spears

1 (10-ounce) box frozen artichoke hearts, thawed

½ teaspoon salt

¼ teaspoon coarsely ground black pepper

1. Combine the lemon juice, wine, garlic, oil, and rosemary in a zip-close plastic bag; add the chicken, potatoes, and artichoke hearts. Squeeze out the air and seal the bag; turn to coat the chicken. Marinate, turning bag occasionally, at room temperature, 30 minutes.

2. Preheat the oven to 450°F. Transfer the chicken, potatoes, and artichoke hearts to a baking dish large enough to hold everything in a single layer. Season with the salt and pepper and spray with olive-oil nonstick spray. Roast until the potatoes are browned and the chicken is cooked through, 20–30 minutes.

Per serving (1 chicken breast and ¼ of vegetables): 400 Cal, 6 g Fat, 1 g Sat Fat, 99 mg Chol, 344 mg Sod, 40 g Carb, 7 g Fib, 44 g Prot, 66 mg Calc. *POINTS* value: *8.*

such a comfort

# Garlic and Thyme Roasted Chicken

**MAKES 4 SERVINGS**

Here's another version of our favorite comfort-style chicken, this time with roasted garlic and fresh thyme tucked under the skin. The bird is served with a light pan gravy prepared with apple juice and just a touch of brown sugar.

12 garlic cloves
1 tablespoon thyme leaves
1 tablespoon olive oil
3/4 teaspoon salt
1/4 teaspoon + 1/8 teaspoon freshly ground pepper
1 (3 1/2–4 pound) chicken
1 cup low-sodium chicken broth
1/2 cup apple juice
2 tablespoons packed dark brown sugar

1. Preheat the oven to 350°F. Wrap the garlic cloves in foil and bake until softened, about 45 minutes; let cool 10 minutes, then remove foil.

2. Increase oven temperature to 375°F. Place a roasting rack inside a roasting pan.

3. Squeeze the garlic pulp into a food processor, discarding the peels. Add the thyme, oil, 1/2 teaspoon of the salt, and 1/4 teaspoon of the pepper to the garlic; puree to form a paste. Gently lift the skin from the breast of the chicken; push the paste under the skin, spreading to cover the meat.

4. Place the chicken, breast-side up, on the rack; tuck the wings behind the chicken. Roast until an instant-read thermometer inserted into the thigh registers 180°F, about 1 hour. Transfer the chicken to a plate, wrap it in foil, and let stand while you make the sauce.

5. Pour the pan juices into a glass measuring cup and skim the fat. Transfer the juices to a small saucepan. Add the broth and apple juice; bring to a boil and boil until reduced to about 3/4 cup, about 10 minutes. Then stir in the brown sugar and the remaining 1/4 teaspoon of salt and 1/8 teaspoon of pepper. Carve the chicken, removing the skin before eating. Serve with the sauce on the side.

Per serving (1/4 chicken with about 3 tablespoons sauce): 309 Cal, 12 g Fat, 3 g Sat Fat, 102 mg Chol, 566 mg Sod, 14 g Carb, 1 g Fib, 34 g Prot, 55 mg Calc. *POINTS* value: **7.**

meals in minutes

# Individual Shepherd's Pies

**MAKES 4 SERVINGS**

These hearty pies are prepared with turkey tenderloin (versus lamb) and feature a whipped potato topping instead of the more highly caloric pastry crust. If you don't have ovenproof soup crocks (or if yours are smaller than 1½ cups), it's just as easy to make one large pie in a two-quart casserole.

2 cups low-sodium chicken broth

1 pound turkey breast tenderloin, cut into 1-inch pieces

1 (10-ounce) package frozen baby peas, thawed

1 (8-ounce) bag yellow pearl onions, peeled

2 carrots, diced

4 teaspoons unsalted butter

3 tablespoons all-purpose flour

1 tablespoon Old Bay seasoning

2 Yukon Gold potatoes, peeled, cubed, and cooked

½ cup low-fat buttermilk

½ teaspoon salt

¼ teaspoon freshly ground pepper

**1.** Preheat the oven to 350°F.

**2.** In a large saucepan, bring the broth to a boil. Add the turkey and poach until no longer pink, about 1 minute. Add the peas, onions, and carrots; bring back to a boil, then cover and remove from the heat.

**3.** In a small skillet, melt the butter over medium heat. Stir in the flour; cook until the flour is brown and begins to smell nutty. Add ½ cup of the poaching liquid and stir until smooth, then stir in the Old Bay seasoning. Transfer this mixture to the saucepan, stirring to blend. Divide the turkey, vegetables, and sauce mixture among 4 (1½-cup) ovenproof soup crocks.

**4.** In a bowl, mash the potatoes until smooth; stir in the buttermilk, salt, and pepper. Spread the mashed potatoes over the turkey mixture. Bake until the potatoes are brown and the filling is bubbling, about 25 minutes.

Per serving (1 pie): 373 Cal, 6 g Fat, 3 g Sat Fat, 84 mg Chol, 1,040 mg Sod, 41 g Carb, 6 g Fib, 37 g Prot, 101 mg Calc. *POINTS* value: *7.*

To cook the potato cubes quickly, place them in a covered microwavable dish along with 2 tablespoons water, and microwave on High until the potatoes are fork-tender, about 3 minutes.

such a comfort

# Cornish Hens with Apricot Sauce

### MAKES 4 SERVINGS

Serve this with rice pilaf or risotto and a simple vegetable, such as roasted Brussels sprouts or sautéed green beans. For a more traditional and slightly sweeter sauce, use ruby port instead of coffee liqueur. Cornish hens are also great for entertaining, so leave the birds whole for a more dramatic presentation. Roast whole birds at 350°F for about 1 hour (an instant-read thermometer inserted into thigh should register 180°F).

½ cup orange juice
¼ cup + 2 tablespoons coffee liqueur
¼ cup apricot preserves
2 tablespoons balsamic vinegar
2 tablespoons Dijon mustard
2 (1½-pound) Cornish hens, quartered

1. Preheat the oven to 450°F. In a small saucepan, combine the orange juice, liqueur, and preserves; bring to a boil. Cook, stirring, until the preserves melt, 1–2 minutes. Reduce the heat and simmer until syrupy, about 4 minutes. Remove from the heat and stir in the vinegar and mustard. Transfer ¼ cup of the sauce to a small bowl.

2. Gently lift the skin from the meat on each hen; brush 1 tablespoon of the sauce from the bowl under the skin of each. Place the hens in a single layer in a roasting pan. Roast until cooked through, about 25 minutes.

3. Just before serving, bring the sauce back to a boil. Place 2 pieces of hen on each of 4 plates; spoon sauce over each.

Per serving (½ hen with about 3 tablespoons sauce): 296 Cal, 5 g Fat, 1 g Sat Fat, 103 mg Chol, 279 mg Sod, 30 g Carb, 0 g Fib, 24 g Prot, 34 mg Calc. *POINTS* value: *6.*

COOK TO COOK

Transferring ¼ cup of the sauce to a bowl before brushing it onto the raw hens helps to avoid contaminating the rest of the sauce with harmful bacteria.

meals in minutes

Cornish Hens with Apricot Sauce

# Warm Cassoulet Salad

**MAKES 6 SERVINGS**

This satisfying salad boasts the main ingredients of a classic French cassoulet—beans, pork, and sausage—but with a fraction of the fat and calories. Prefer home-cooked beans to canned? Soak 1 cup dried beans overnight; to cook, cover with water and boil until tender, about one hour. Use green cabbage in place of red (or a combo) if you wish.

4 teaspoons olive oil

$\frac{1}{2}$ pound pork tenderloin, trimmed of all visible fat and cut into $\frac{1}{2}$-inch chunks

1 large white onion, chopped

4 large garlic cloves, minced

$\frac{1}{2}$ cup dry white wine

$\frac{1}{4}$ cup sliced oil-packed sun-dried tomatoes, drained and patted dry

2 teaspoons thyme leaves

2 teaspoons rosemary leaves

$\frac{1}{4}$ pound smoked turkey sausage, thinly sliced

2 (15-ounce) cans Great Northern beans, rinsed and drained

1 small red cabbage, cored and chopped

1 teaspoon grated lemon zest

2 tablespoons chopped fresh parsley

1 teaspoon salt

$\frac{1}{4}$ teaspoon coarsely ground black pepper

**1.** Heat 2 teaspoons of the oil in a large straight-sided skillet over medium-high heat. Add the pork and cook until browned. Add the onion and garlic and cook until the onion has softened. Add the wine, sun-dried tomatoes, thyme, and rosemary and cook 1 minute, then stir in the sausage and beans. Cover, reduce the heat, and simmer until the flavors are blended, about 15 minutes.

**2.** Add the cabbage and lemon zest to the skillet. Increase the heat to medium and cook until the cabbage is slightly wilted. Stir in the parsley, salt, pepper, and the remaining 2 teaspoons oil.

Per serving (1$\frac{1}{3}$ cups): 253 Cal, 7 g Fat, 2 g Sat Fat, 37 mg Chol, 935 mg Sod, 31 g Carb, 10 g Fib, 20 g Prot, 140 mg Calc. **POINTS** value: **5.**

meals in minutes

# Duck Breast and Wild Mushroom Gratin

**MAKES 6 SERVINGS**

Lots of meaty, mildly peppery oyster mushrooms enhance this soothing, quiche-like dish. The Madeira, a fortified Spanish wine, complements the duck and boosts the richness of the gratin. Be sure to use lean Muscovy duck, which contains only a fraction of the fat of other varieties.

½ tablespoon olive oil

1 large Vidalia onion, sliced

1 (6-ounce) package oyster mushrooms, trimmed

4 large red chard leaves, sliced

2 tablespoons Madeira

1 (6-ounce) skinless Muscovy duck breast, cut into strips

3 large eggs

¾ cup fat-free egg substitute

½ teaspoon salt

¼ teaspoon coarsely ground black pepper

**1.** Preheat the oven to 350°F. Spray a 9-inch quiche pan with nonstick spray.

**2.** Heat the oil in a nonstick skillet over medium-high heat. Add the onion and cook, stirring, until it begins to turn golden. Add the mushrooms, chard, and Madeira and cook 3 minutes longer. Add the duck and cook until it is no longer pink. Scrape mixture into the quiche pan.

**3.** Mix together the eggs, egg substitute, salt, and pepper. Pour over the contents of the quiche pan. Bake until the gratin is browned on top, about 25 minutes. Remove from oven and let stand 10 minutes, then cut into 6 wedges.

Per serving (1 wedge): 111 Cal, 5 g Fat, 1 g Sat Fat, 128 mg Chol, 320 mg Sod, 4 g Carb, 1 g Fib, 11 g Prot, 33 mg Calc. *POINTS* value: *2.*

such a comfort

# Turkey and Spinach Lasagna Rolls

**MAKES 6 SERVINGS**

These unique cheese-and-spinach-stuffed lasagna bundles, smothered in a turkey marinara sauce, are easy to serve and bound to be a favorite with kids and adults alike. They also supply built-in portion control.

- **6 lasagna noodles**
- **1 teaspoon olive oil**
- **$\frac{1}{2}$ pound ground skinless turkey breast**
- **1 onion, chopped**
- **1 yellow bell pepper, seeded and finely chopped**
- **1 (16-ounce) container refrigerated fresh marinara sauce**
- **$\frac{1}{3}$ cup water**
- **1 cup fat-free ricotta cheese**
- **$\frac{1}{2}$ (10-ounce) package frozen chopped spinach, thawed and squeezed dry**
- **$\frac{1}{4}$ cup chopped fresh basil**
- **2 tablespoons grated Parmesan cheese**
- **1 large egg, lightly beaten**
- **$\frac{1}{8}$ teaspoon ground nutmeg**
- **$\frac{1}{2}$ cup shredded part-skim mozzarella cheese**

1. Cook the lasagna noodles according to package directions. Drain and rinse the noodles and lay them flat on wax paper.

2. Heat oil in a large nonstick skillet over medium-high heat. Add the turkey, onion, and bell pepper and cook, stirring frequently, until all the pan juices evaporate and the turkey browns, about 10 minutes. Stir in the marinara sauce and water; bring to a boil. Reduce the heat and simmer, uncovered, until slightly thickened and the flavors blend, about 5 minutes.

3. Preheat the oven to 375°F. Meanwhile, combine the ricotta, spinach, basil, Parmesan, egg, and nutmeg in a medium bowl. Spread the ricotta mixture over the length of each noodle and roll up from one short end.

4. Spread half of the turkey mixture in the bottom of an 8 x 12-inch baking dish. Add the rolls. Top with the remaining turkey mixture. Cover with foil and bake 30 minutes. Remove the foil and sprinkle with the mozzarella. Bake until heated through and the top is golden, about 10 minutes longer.

Per serving (1 roll with $\frac{1}{6}$ of sauce): 277 Cal, 9 g Fat, 3 g Sat Fat, 65 mg Chol, 496 mg Sod, 27 g Carb, 3 g Fib, 23 g Prot, 228 mg Calc. ***POINTS*** value: *6.*

Turkey and
Spinach
Lasagna Rolls

# Beef Ragout on Polenta Cakes

**MAKES 6 SERVINGS**

This variation on a northern Italian tradition features meaty beef cubes instead of the typical ground beef, uses hearty red wine in place of white, and boasts rich Mission figs. A Chianti would be in keeping with the dish's roots, but any dry red wine will do. Many supermarkets stock precooked polenta logs; look in the pasta aisle or near produce, in the refrigerator section. These logs are virtually fat-free and very convenient.

½ tablespoon olive oil

1 small yellow onion, chopped

1 celery stalk, chopped

1 carrot, chopped

2 garlic cloves, chopped

1 pound beef top round steak, trimmed of all visible fat and cut into ½-inch cubes

1 cup dry red wine

1½ tablespoons chopped fresh basil, or ½ tablespoon dried

1 tablespoon chopped fresh thyme, or 1 teaspoon dried

1 (14½-ounce) can diced tomatoes

1 tablespoon tomato paste

9 dried Mission figs, chopped

½ teaspoon salt

¼ teaspoon coarsely ground black pepper

1 (1-pound) log plain polenta, cut into 12 (½-inch) slices

**1.** Heat oil in a nonstick Dutch oven over medium-high heat. Add the onion, celery, carrot, and garlic and cook, stirring, until the onion softens. Add the beef and cook until browned. Stir in the wine and cook over high heat, scraping up the browned bits from the bottom of the pan, until the liquid is reduced by one-half, 3–4 minutes. Add the basil, thyme, and tomatoes and bring back to a boil. Cover, reduce the heat, and simmer until the meat is very tender, about 35 minutes.

**2.** Stir in the tomato paste, figs, salt, and pepper. Cook, uncovered, until mixture thickens, about 10 minutes longer.

**3.** Meanwhile, spray a broiler rack with nonstick spray; preheat the broiler. Broil the polenta slices 5 inches from the heat until lightly browned, about 2 minutes on each side. Serve the ragout ladled over the polenta.

Per serving (generous 1 cup stew with 2 slices polenta): 363 Cal, 4 g Fat, 1 g Sat Fat, 43 mg Chol, 812 mg Sod, 52 g Carb, 7 g Fib, 22 g Prot, 94 mg Calc. *POINTS* value: *7.*

# Choucroute Garni

**MAKES 4 SERVINGS**

In France, *choucroute,* the French word for sauerkraut, is traditionally cooked with onions, juniper berries or caraway seeds, and plenty of goose fat. Thankfully this version skips the goose, thus providing only a fraction of the fat! The pork and sauerkraut in this recipe are a natural combination that apples only serve to improve. For best flavor use the sauerkraut found in plastic bags in the supermarket refrigerator section rather than the bottled or canned variety.

1 tablespoon Dijon mustard

2 teaspoons thyme leaves

1 teaspoon packed dark brown sugar

1 garlic clove, minced

1/2 teaspoon salt

1/2 teaspoon freshly ground pepper

1–1 1/4 pounds pork tenderloin, trimmed of all visible fat

2 ounces smoked turkey sausage, chopped

1 small white onion, minced

1 Granny Smith apple, cored and grated

1 cup apple cider vinegar

1 pound sauerkraut, rinsed and squeezed dry

1. Preheat the oven to 350°F. In a small bowl mix the mustard, 1 teaspoon of the thyme, the brown sugar, garlic, salt, and pepper. Coat the tenderloin with the mixture and place it in a shallow roasting pan. Roast until the pork reaches an internal temperature of 160°F, about 30 minutes. Transfer to a cutting board and let stand 10 minutes before slicing.

2. Meanwhile, in a medium saucepan brown the sausage about 5 minutes. Stir in the onion, apple, and the remaining 1 teaspoon thyme; cook, covered, until the onion is softened, about 5 minutes. Add the vinegar and cook until it is reduced by half, about 5 minutes. Stir in the sauerkraut and cook until the liquid is absorbed, about 5 minutes longer.

3. Slice the tenderloin into 1/2-inch medallions. Fan the medallions on 4 plates and serve with the sauerkraut.

Per serving (4 [1-ounce] slices pork with about 1 cup sauerkraut): 263 Cal, 8 g Fat, 2 g Sat Fat, 102 mg Chol, 1,390 mg Sod, 14 g Carb, 5 g Fib, 34 g Prot, 75 mg Calc. *POINTS* value: *5.*

such a comfort

# Roast Pork with Herb Crust

**MAKES 6 SERVINGS**

This intensely flavorful dish derives its character from a combination of thyme, coarse salt, and pepper. The hot oven temperature sears the roast, producing a crusty outside yet leaving the inside juicy and tender. Be sure to sprinkle some of the seasoning mixture over the onion and apple base.

1 tablespoon dried thyme

2 teaspoons coarse salt

$3/4$ teaspoon coarsely ground black pepper

1 large Vidalia onion, thinly sliced

2 small Granny Smith apples, cored and thinly sliced

1 ($1^3/4$–2-pound) boneless pork top loin roast, trimmed of all visible fat

**1.** Preheat the oven to 450°F. Mix together the thyme, salt, and pepper. Scatter the onion and apples over the bottom of a rectangular roasting pan and sprinkle with $1/2$ tablespoon of the seasoning mixture. Place the roast on top and rub the exposed surface with the rest of the seasoning mixture. Roast 15 minutes.

**2.** Reduce the oven temperature to 300°F and roast until the pork reaches an internal temperature of 155°F, 35–40 minutes. Remove from the oven and let stand 10 minutes before slicing. Serve with the apples and onion on the side.

Per serving (about 5 slices pork and $1/3$ cup apples and onions): 210 Cal, 5 g Fat, 2 g Sat Fat, 98 mg Chol, 704 mg Sod, 8 g Carb, 1 g Fib, 32 g Prot, 27 mg Calc. **POINTS** value: **4.**

We like Granny Smith apples because their tart flavor contrasts well with the richness of the pork and they hold their shape. But other apples would work well, too. Try McIntoshes (peel them first) for a sweeter flavor to balance the onion; these will cook down into an applesauce-like consistency.

# Veal Stew Italiano

**MAKES 6 SERVINGS**

Serve this elegant, flavorsome stew over hearty pasta (like penne or rigatoni) or soft polenta, garnished with shavings of Parmigiano-Reggiano cheese. A red wine like Chianti or merlot pairs well with this dish on a winter's night.

- 2 teaspoons extra-virgin olive oil
- $^3/_4$ pound veal top round, trimmed of all visible fat and cut into $^1/_4$-inch cubes
- 1 carrot, minced
- 1 celery stalk, minced
- 1 white onion, minced
- 2 garlic cloves, minced
- $^1/_2$ cup dry white wine
- 1 (28-ounce) can diced tomatoes in juice
- 1 bay leaf
- $^3/_4$ teaspoon dried oregano, crumbled
- $^1/_2$ teaspoon salt
- $^1/_8$ teaspoon crushed red pepper

**1.** Heat the oil in a Dutch oven over medium-high heat. Add the veal and cook, stirring, until no longer pink, 2–3 minutes. Add the carrot, celery, onion, and garlic; cook until the vegetables are soft, 8–10 minutes.

**2.** Pour in the wine, increase the heat to high, and cook until the wine is reduced to about 2 tablespoons, about 5 minutes. Stir in the tomatoes, bay leaf, oregano, salt, and red pepper. Reduce the heat and simmer, covered, until the meat is very tender and the sauce is very thick, about 1–1$^1/_4$ hours. Discard the bay leaf.

Per serving (about 1$^1/_4$ cups): 130 Cal, 4 g Fat, 1 g Sat Fat, 45 mg Chol, 268 mg Sod, 8 g Carb, 2 g Fib, 13 g Prot, 31 mg Calc. **_POINTS_** value: **_3._**

Cook with white wine but serve with red? Yes, indeed: Veal should be cooked with white wine because red would be too overpowering. But tomato-based stews should be served with a medium-bodied red.

# Moroccan Turkey-Ham Tagine

**MAKES 4 SERVINGS**

Tagines are traditional Moroccan stews, often served with couscous. This one is presented in the traditional style, mounded in a well of couscous. Although we often think of curry powder as an Indian seasoning blend, it contains all of the spices integral to Middle Eastern cooking, as well.

1 **pound turkey ham, trimmed and cut into** $^3/_4$**-inch cubes**

1 **teaspoon curry powder**

$^1/_2$ **teaspoon ground cinnamon**

$^1/_2$ **teaspoon ground ginger**

$^1/_2$ **tablespoon olive oil**

1 **garlic clove, chopped**

2 **cups low-sodium beef broth**

1 **large sweet potato, cut into** $^3/_4$**-inch chunks**

1 **large white onion, cut into** $^3/_4$**-inch chunks**

15 **pitted prunes, halved**

1 **(3 x** $^1/_2$**-inch) strip lemon zest**

$1^1/_2$ **cups water**

1 **cup couscous**

$^1/_2$ **teaspoon ground coriander**

$^1/_8$ **teaspoon ground turmeric (optional)**

2 **tablespoons slivered almonds**

2 **tablespoons chopped fresh cilantro**

**1.** Combine the turkey ham, curry powder, cinnamon, and ginger in a bowl and toss to coat the meat.

**2.** Heat the oil in a nonstick Dutch oven over medium heat. Add the garlic and cook, stirring, until fragrant. Add the turkey ham and cook until lightly browned. Add the broth, scraping up the browned bits from the bottom of the pan. Bring to a boil, then stir in the sweet potato, onion, prunes, and lemon zest. Cover, reduce the heat, and simmer, stirring after 20 minutes, until the sweet potato and onion are tender, about 30 minutes.

**3.** To make the couscous, bring the water to a boil in a small saucepan. Remove the pot from the heat and stir in the couscous, coriander, turmeric (if using), and almonds. Cover and set aside to steep at least 5 minutes. Stir in the cilantro. Spoon the couscous onto a platter, making a well in the center, and mound the tagine inside the well.

Per serving (about 1 cup tagine and $^3/_4$ cup couscous): 399 Cal, 12 g Fat, 3 g Sat Fat, 78 mg Chol, 1,164 mg Sod, 51 g Carb, 6 g Fib, 25 g Prot, 89 mg Calc. **POINTS** value: **8.**

Turkey ham is turkey that has been processed to taste like ham. It contains considerably less fat than most of the meats typically used in stews. Because it is precooked, it also cuts preparation time to a fraction.

meals in minutes

Moroccan
Turkey-Ham
Tagine

# Fish Chowder Pie in a Bacon Biscuit Crust

**MAKES 6 SERVINGS**

If you love comfy fish chowders, this is the perfect one-dish meal. Haddock, halibut, or sea bass make good replacements for the cod. The filling may be made ahead and refrigerated overnight, then brought back to room temperature before baking.

**Filling:**
- ½ tablespoon olive oil
- 1 large white onion, chopped
- 1 large red potato, peeled and chopped
- 2 carrots, chopped
- 2 celery stalks, chopped
- 2 garlic cloves, minced
- 1 cup clam juice
- 1¾ cups water
- 1 teaspoon chopped rosemary
- ½ cup fat-free half-and-half
- 2 teaspoons Dijon mustard
- 1 tablespoon Worcestershire sauce
- 3 tablespoons cornstarch
- 1½ pounds cod fillets, cut into 1-inch chunks
- ¼ cup chopped seeded red bell pepper
- ½ tablespoon chopped thyme
- ⅔ cup fresh or thawed frozen corn kernels
- 1 teaspoon salt
- ½ teaspoon coarsely ground black pepper

**Crust:**
- 2 cups all-purpose flour
- 2 teaspoons baking powder
- ½ teaspoon salt
- 3 tablespoons cold butter
- ¾ cup low-fat buttermilk
- 4 strips crisp-cooked turkey bacon, crumbled

**1.** To make the filling, heat oil in a large heavy-bottomed saucepan. Add the onion, potato, carrots, celery, and garlic and cook, stirring, 2 minutes. Add the clam juice, water, and rosemary. Bring to a boil, then reduce the heat and simmer, stirring occasionally, until the vegetables are tender, about 10 minutes.

**2.** In a small bowl mix together the half-and-half, mustard, Worcestershire sauce, and cornstarch. Stir the mixture into the saucepan, then add the cod, bell pepper, thyme, corn, salt, and ground pepper. Simmer, uncovered, until the fish is opaque, about 5 minutes.

**3.** Preheat the oven to 400°F. Pour the fish mixture into a round 2-quart baking dish and set dish on a baking sheet.

**4.** To make the crust, combine the flour, baking powder, and salt in a bowl. Cut the butter into pieces, then cut into mixture with a fork or a pastry blender until mixture is crumbly. Stir in the buttermilk and bacon. Gather the dough into a ball. On a lightly floured counter, roll out the dough into a 10-inch circle, about ¼-inch thick. Fit the dough over the baking dish and crimp the excess around the rim to seal. Poke all over with the tines of a fork. Bake until the crust is puffed and browned and the filling is bubbling, about 30 minutes.

Per serving (⅙ of pie): 292 Cal, 10 g Fat, 5 g Sat Fat, 74 mg Chol, 671 mg Sod, 25 g Carb, 2 g Fib, 25 g Prot, 92 mg Calc. *POINTS* value: *6.*

meals in minutes

# Salmon Persillade with Zesty Mashed Potatoes

**MAKES 4 SERVINGS**

*Persillade*, a sprightly combination of parsley and garlic, is mixed with bread crumbs and lemon to make a delicious crunchy topping for salmon. To round out the meal, serve a vitamin-and-mineral-rich green vegetable, such as steamed broccoli.

8 cups water

1 pound red potatoes, peeled and quartered

1 pound salmon fillet, cut into 4 pieces

4 teaspoons Dijon mustard

1/4 cup plain dried bread crumbs

1 tablespoon chopped fresh parsley

1 garlic clove, minced

2 teaspoons grated lemon zest

1 teaspoon olive oil

3/4 teaspoon salt

1/3 cup low-fat (1%) milk

3 tablespoons light sour cream

2 tablespoons prepared horseradish

Parsley sprigs

**1.** Bring the water and potatoes to a boil in a large saucepan. Reduce the heat and simmer, covered, until the potatoes are fork-tender, about 20 minutes. Drain and keep warm.

**2.** Preheat the oven to 425°F. Spray a baking sheet with nonstick spray. Place the salmon pieces on the baking sheet; brush the tops with the mustard.

**3.** Combine the bread crumbs, parsley, garlic, lemon zest, oil, and 1/4 teaspoon of the salt in a bowl. Sprinkle the bread-crumb mixture on top of the salmon; spray lightly with nonstick spray. Bake until salmon is just opaque in the center and topping is golden brown, about 15 minutes.

**4.** Meanwhile, transfer the potatoes to a large bowl; add the milk, sour cream, horseradish, and the remaining 1/2 teaspoon salt. Beat, with an electric mixer on medium speed until the potatoes are smooth and creamy. Serve with the salmon and garnish with the parsley sprigs.

Per serving (1 piece salmon and 1/2 cup potatoes): 318 Cal, 9 g Fat, 3 g Sat Fat, 79 mg Chol, 662 mg Sod, 29 g Carb, 2 g Fib, 29 g Prot, 90 mg Calc. *POINTS* value. *7.*

COOK TO COOK

If you like your spuds chunky, leave the skins on the potatoes and mash with a potato masher or the back of a wooden spoon.

such a comfort

# Paella Valenciana

**MAKES 8 SERVINGS**

This traditional dish from the Valencia region of Spain can be a real showstopper when you serve it in the authentic Spanish manner: Bring it to the table in a paella pan, garnished with flat-leaf parsley and lemon wedges. Lacking a paella pan, you can use a skillet, at least 12 inches but preferably 14 to 15 inches, with ovenproof handles.

3½ cups low-sodium
   chicken broth
⅛ teaspoon saffron threads
⅛ teaspoon cayenne,
   or to taste
2 teaspoons olive oil
1 white onion, chopped
2 garlic cloves, chopped
1 pound medium shrimp,
   peeled and deveined
1 pound skinless boneless
   chicken breasts, cubed
2 cups Arborio or other
   short-grained rice
½ cup dry white wine
¼ pound smoked turkey
   sausage, thinly sliced
1 pound asparagus,
   steamed and cut into
   1-inch lengths

**1.** Preheat the oven to 325°F. In a medium saucepan, combine the broth, saffron, and cayenne; bring to a boil.

**2.** Meanwhile, heat the oil in a very large nonstick skillet or paella pan over medium-high heat. Add the onion and garlic and cook, stirring, until they begin to color, about 2 minutes. Add the shrimp and the chicken; cook until the shrimp turn pink and the chicken begins to brown, about 1 minute. Add the rice and cook, stirring, 1 minute. Add the broth mixture and the wine, then stir in the sausage and asparagus; bring back to a boil. Reduce the heat to medium and cook 5 minutes.

**3.** Transfer the pan to the oven. Bake until the liquid is absorbed and the rice is tender, about 15 minutes. Serve at once.

Per serving (scant 1½ cups): 379 Cal, 6 g Fat, 2 g Sat Fat, 131 mg Chol, 281 mg Sod, 45 g Carb, 3 g Fib, 33 g Prot, 66 mg Calc. **POINTS** value: **7**.

such a comfort

# Sea Bass Wellington

**MAKES 6 SERVINGS**

Remember Beef Wellington? It was a popular dinner-party dish in the fifties and sixties that consisted of a fillet of beef coated with foie gras and wrapped in puff pastry. Our healthy version is stuffed with sea bass instead of beef, and a rich mushroom pâté replaces the foie gras. Tuna, monkfish, or any firm-fleshed white fish, such as halibut or cod, could stand in for the sea bass. Replace the white mushrooms with any combination of portobellos, shiitakes, and cremini, if you desire.

1 (1-pound) package white mushrooms, courseley chopped
½ teaspoon dried thyme
½ teaspoon salt
½ teaspoon coarsely ground black pepper
½ cup fat-free half-and-half
1 (5 x 10-inch) piece thawed frozen puff pastry (½ sheet)
1 pound sea bass fillets, skin removed

**1.** Spray a large nonstick skillet with olive-oil nonstick spray and set over medium-high heat. Add the mushrooms and cook, stirring, until all of the liquid evaporates, about 5 minutes. Stir in the thyme, salt, pepper, and half-and-half. Reduce the heat and simmer, uncovered, until the mushrooms are very soft and most of the half-and-half is absorbed, about 15 minutes. Transfer the contents of the pan to a food processor or blender and puree, scraping down the sides midway through if necessary. Cover and freeze for 45 minutes.

**2.** Preheat the oven to 400°F. On a lightly floured surface, roll out the puff pastry into an 8½ x 11-inch rectangle. Leaving a ½-inch border all around, spread the chilled mushroom puree over the dough. Lay the fillets down the center. Fold the dough up around the fish and pinch closed. Gently transfer to a foil- or parchment-lined baking sheet, placing seam-side down. Spray with olive-oil nonstick spray and bake until well puffed and golden, about 30 minutes. Transfer to a platter and let stand 5 minutes before cutting into 6 slices.

Per serving (1 slice): 159 Cal, 5 g Fat, 1 g Sat Fat, 31 mg Chol, 281 mg Sod, 10 g Carb, 1 g Fib, 17 g Prot, 12 mg Calc. *POINTS* value: *3.*

meals in minutes

Sea Bass
Wellington

# life is sweet!

YUMMY DELIGHTS TO SATISFY ALL
YOUR DESSERT DESIRES

# Chocolate Cherry Biscotti

**MAKES 30 SERVINGS**

Cherries and chocolate are a classic combination, so we added candied cherries to crisp, chocolatey biscotti. Candied cherries are sometimes called glacé cherries and have been dried, then coated with sugar syrup. If you prefer, you can replace them with an equal amount of dried cherries, raisins, or whole almonds.

1 cup fat-free egg substitute
¼ cup packed dark brown sugar
4 teaspoons vanilla extract
2 cups all-purpose flour
1 cup + 2 tablespoons unsweetened Dutch processed cocoa
¾ cup granulated sugar
2 teaspoons baking powder
½ teaspoon salt
1¼ cups candied cherries

**1.** Preheat the oven to 350°F. Line a large baking sheet with parchment paper, nonstick plastic ovenware liner, or wax paper.

**2.** In a small bowl, combine the egg substitute, brown sugar, and vanilla; whisk until frothy. In a large bowl, combine the flour, cocoa, granulated sugar, baking powder, and salt. Stir in the cherries, then add the egg mixture and stir to form a dough.

**3.** Transfer the dough to a lightly floured work surface and divide it in half. Transfer the halves to the baking sheet and with floured hands form each into a long, thin loaf about ¾-inch high. Bake until well risen and firm to the touch, 25–35 minutes. Cut the loaves into 30 (¾-inch) slices; arrange the slices, flat-side down, on the baking sheet. Bake 10 minutes, turn, and bake until crisp and dry to the touch on both sides, 10 minutes more. Cool the slices on wire racks.

Per serving (1 biscotti): 82 Cal, 1 g Fat, 0 g Sat Fat, 0 mg Chol, 71 mg Sod, 17 g Carb, 2 g Fib, 3 g Prot, 13 mg Calc. **POINTS** value: **1.**

To gild the lily, melt 2 ounces white chocolate in a small glass measuring cup, and with a small spoon drizzle it over the cooled biscotti.

# Ginger Crisp Cookies

**MAKES 24 SERVINGS**

Despite the tablespoon of ground ginger, these crispy cookies actually have a fairly subtle flavor. To boost the spiciness, replace up to 3 tablespoons of the ½ cup granulated sugar used in the cookie dough with dark brown sugar; this will also produce a slightly chewier cookie.

- 1 **cup all-purpose flour**
- 1 **tablespoon ground ginger**
- ½ **teaspoon ground cinnamon**
- ¼ **teaspoon baking soda**
- ¼ **teaspoon salt**
- ⅛ **teaspoon ground allspice**
- ¾ **cup sugar**
- 4 **tablespoons unsalted butter, at room temperature**
- 1 **large egg**
- 2 **tablespoons dark molasses**

1. Preheat the oven to 350°F. In a medium bowl whisk the flour, ginger, cinnamon, baking soda, salt, and allspice. Reserve ¼ cup of the sugar in a small bowl.

2. In a large bowl, with an electric mixer on medium speed, cream the remaining ½ cup sugar and the butter. Mix in the egg and molasses, continuing to beat until combined. Mix in the dry ingredients. Drop dough onto baking sheets by the tablespoonful, leaving 2–3 inches between cookies, making 24 cookies. Spray the bottom of a 2½-inch glass with nonstick spray. Dip it into the bowl of reserved sugar and flatten a mound of dough. Continue to dip and flatten the remainder of the cookie dough. Bake until the cookies are firm to the touch and lightly colored around the edges, 10–12 minutes. Cool on the baking sheet on a wire rack 10 minutes, then remove the cookies from baking sheet and cool completely on rack.

Per serving (1 cookie): 68 Cal, 2 g Fat, 1 g Sat Fat, 13 mg Chol, 41 mg Sod, 12 g Carb, 0 g Fib, 1 g Prot, 7 mg Calc. **POINTS** value: **2.**

life is sweet!

 For slightly sweeter cookies, roll each tablespoonful of dough in the reserved sugar before placing onto the baking sheet; flatten each with a plain glass.

Lemon-Nut Tuiles and
Cappuccino Sorbet

# Lemon-Nut Tuiles

## MAKES 12 SERVINGS

*Tuiles* (pronounced "tweel"), the French word for tiles, are thin, crisp cookies that resemble the shape of a curved roof tile. While still warm they're draped over a rolling pin to create their characteristic curved shape. Serve these with sorbet [like our Cappuccino Sorbet on the next page], fresh berries, or simply a cup of freshly brewed coffee.

½ cup sugar
3 tablespoons butter
½ teaspoon almond extract
2 egg whites
1 tablespoon grated lemon zest
⅓ cup all-purpose flour
¼ cup sliced almonds, coarsely chopped

1. Preheat the oven to 400°F. Spray a large baking sheet with nonstick spray. Line with parchment paper.
2. Pulse the sugar, butter, and almond extract in a food processor until just mixed, about 20 seconds. Add the egg whites and lemon zest; pulse until just blended, about 15 seconds longer. Add the flour and process until just blended, about 10 seconds. Transfer the mixture to a bowl; stir in the almonds.
3. Working in batches, drop rounded tablespoonfuls of the batter onto the baking sheet. Spread the batter out very thinly with the back of a spoon into 4-inch rounds, about 1 inch apart. You will get about 4 cookies on each sheet.
4. Bake until the cookies are lightly browned and the edges are dry, about 10 minutes. Cool on the baking sheet about 1 minute. Then, using a small knife or metal spatula, lift the cookies and place them over a rolling pin to give them a curved shape, until set, about 10 minutes. Repeat with the remaining batter, making a total of 12 cookies. Store the cookies in an airtight container for up to 3 days.

Per serving (1 cookie): 85 Cal, 4 g Fat, 2 g Sat Fat, 8 mg Chol, 29 mg Sod, 12 g Carb, 0 g Fib, 1 g Prot, 7 mg Calc. **POINTS** value: **2.**

life is sweet!

COOK TO COOK

It's important to work fast, since the cookies may begin to harden too quickly. If the cookies do harden before they are shaped, pop them back into the hot oven for a few seconds to soften before draping over the rolling pin. Or you can simply roll them into little cigarette shapes.

# Cappuccino Sorbet

**MAKES 8 SERVINGS**

Easy to make (no ice cream machine required!), this sorbet will cool you off on the hottest of days. Partially frozen in a shallow pan and whirled to a creamy smooth consistency in a food processor, it's a snap to make.

3 cups water
1 cup sugar
$^3/_4$ cup unsweetened cocoa powder
$^3/_4$ cup light corn syrup
2 (1-ounce) squares semisweet chocolate, chopped
1 tablespoon instant espresso powder
1 teaspoon ground cinnamon
$^1/_4$ teaspoon ground nutmeg
1 cup fat-free half-and-half

**1.** Bring the water, sugar, cocoa, corn syrup, chocolate, espresso, cinnamon, and nutmeg to a boil in a saucepan. Reduce the heat and simmer until the sugar dissolves, about 5 minutes. Remove from the heat. Stir in the half-and-half. Pour into a 9 x 13-inch baking dish. Cover with plastic wrap and freeze until partially frozen, about 2 hours.

**2.** Working in batches, spoon the sorbet into a food processor or blender. Process 1 minute. Pour back into the baking dish. Cover with plastic wrap and freeze 1 hour.

**3.** Repeat Step 2. Freeze until firm, about $1^1/_2$ hours.

Per serving ($^1/_2$ cup): 228 Cal, 3 g Fat, 2 g Sat Fat, 0 mg Chol, 52 mg Sod, 53 g Carb, 3 g Fib, 3 g Prot, 58 mg Calc. *POINTS* value: *4.*

meals in minutes

# Pineapple and Orange Sorbet

**MAKES 8 SERVINGS**

Even if you usually shun canned fruit, you must try this dessert. Canned fruit makes it almost criminally easy, and you'd never guess you're not eating the freshest fruits. When pureed, the pineapple takes on a pale off-white hue evocative of cream-laden sherbet.

1 (20-ounce) can crushed pineapple in heavy syrup, frozen
1 (8-ounce) can mandarin oranges in light syrup, frozen
1/4 cup packed light brown sugar
1/4 cup golden rum

Open the cans on both ends and push the frozen fruit onto a cutting board. Cut into quarters, then transfer to a food processor and pulse about 20 times to break up. Pulse in the brown sugar. With the machine running, drizzle in the rum; process until smooth, about 20 seconds. Spoon the sorbet into parfait glasses.

Per serving (1/2 cup): 123 Cal, 0 g Fat, 0 g Sat Fat, 0 mg Chol, 5 mg Sod, 28 g Carb, 1 g Fib, 0 g Prot, 19 mg Calc. **POINTS** value: **2.**

life is sweet!

It will take the fruit about 8 to 12 hours to freeze completely. If the frozen fruit does not push out of the can easily, hold the can sideways under hot running water for about 10 seconds, taking care not to moisten the fruit.

# Orange Madeleines

**MAKES 12 SERVINGS**

Madeleines are little shell-shaped cakes, crisp around the edge and spongy inside. They are baked in special molds with scallop-shell-shaped indentations; if you prefer, you can bake mini muffins from this recipe instead. These elegant treats pair deliciously with our Pineapple and Orange Sorbet [see recipe on the previous page].

¼ cup fat-free egg
  substitute
¼ cup + 2 tablespoons
  confectioners' sugar
2 tablespoons unsalted
  butter, melted
1 teaspoon orange liqueur
3 tablespoons all-purpose
  flour
1 teaspoon grated
  orange zest
1 tablespoon chopped
  bittersweet chocolate

**1.** Preheat the oven to 350°F. Spray a 12-shell madeleine mold with nonstick spray.

**2.** In a large bowl, whisk the egg substitute until frothy. Whisk in the confectioners' sugar, butter, and liqueur, then stir in the flour and orange zest. Spoon 1 tablespoon of the batter into each shell of the madeleine mold. Bake until golden brown, 11–12 minutes. Cool in the mold on a wire rack 1 minute, then remove the madeleines from the mold and cool completely on the rack.

**3.** Put the chocolate into a microwavable bowl. Microwave on Medium, stirring every 30 seconds, until melted, about 1½ minutes. Using a small spoon, drizzle the melted chocolate over the cooled madeleines.

Per serving (1 madeleine): 212 Cal, 8 g Fat, 5 g Sat Fat, 24 mg Chol, 322 mg Sod, 25 g Carb, 2 g Fib, 11 g Prot, 95 mg Calc. *POINTS* value: *5.*

Orange Madeleines and
Pineapple and Orange Sorbet

# Banana Cream Crêpes with Chocolate Sauce

**MAKES 4 SERVINGS**

These thin, delicate pancakes can be served with a variety of fillings. If you like, substitute your favorite berries, peaches, or nectarines for the bananas. Or simply spread the crêpes with jam and sprinkle with confectioners' sugar.

½ cup low-fat (1%) milk

¼ cup all-purpose flour

1 large egg

2 teaspoons sugar

Pinch of salt

2 ripe bananas, thinly sliced

1 tablespoon chopped toasted pecans

½ teaspoon ground cinnamon

¾ cup light nondairy whipped topping

¼ cup bottled chocolate sauce

1. To make the crêpes, beat the milk, flour, egg, sugar, and salt in a medium bowl until smooth; let stand 15 minutes.

2. Meanwhile, combine the bananas, toasted pecans, and cinnamon in a bowl. Gently fold in the whipped topping until just blended.

3. Spray a crêpe pan or 6-inch nonstick skillet with nonstick spray and set over medium-high heat until a drop of water sizzles. Pour in one-fourth of the batter and swirl to cover the pan. Cook until the underside is set, about 30 seconds. Flip and cook until lightly browned, about 1 minute longer. Slide the crêpe onto wax paper. Repeat with the remaining batter, making a total of 4 crêpes; stack the crêpes between sheets of wax paper to prevent them from sticking to one another.

4. Top each crêpe with one-quarter of the banana mixture; roll to enclose the filling. Drizzle with the chocolate sauce. Repeat with the remaining crêpes, filling, and sauce.

Per serving (1 filled crêpe with 1 tablespoon chocolate sauce): 201 Cal, 5 g Fat, 2 g Sat Fat, 55 mg Chol, 129 mg Sod, 38 g Carb, 2 g Fib, 5 g Prot, 64 mg Calc. *POINTS* value: **4.**

COOK TO COOK

To have extra crêpes on hand, double the batter. Layer the extras between sheets of wax paper, place in a zip-close bag, and freeze for up to three months. The batter can be made up to a day ahead and refrigerated. Let stand at least 15 minutes before cooking to give the flour time to absorb the liquid.

# Coeur à la Crème with Apricot Sauce

**MAKES 4 SERVINGS**

This light, creamy French dessert is traditionally made in ceramic heart-shaped molds with perforated bottoms to allow any moisture to drain. However, this lighter version needs no special molds. Simply line individual custard cups with dampened cheesecloth to make unmolding easier. You can make this up to a day ahead and refrigerate.

6 ounces fat-free
cream cheese
¼ cup confectioners' sugar
1 teaspoon vanilla extract
¾ cup light nondairy
whipped topping
¾ cup apricot jam
¼ cup water
1 teaspoon fresh
lemon juice
Fresh mint sprigs

**1.** With an electric mixer on high speed, beat the cream cheese, sugar, and vanilla in a medium bowl until blended. Gently fold in the whipped topping.

**2.** Cut a sheet of cheesecloth into 4 (8-inch) squares and dampen slightly with cold water. Line 4 (6-ounce) custard cups with the cheesecloth, allowing the excess to overhang. Spoon the cream cheese mixture into the custard cups. Fold the excess cheesecloth over the tops. Refrigerate until just set, about 2 hours or overnight.

**3.** Bring the jam, water, and lemon juice to a boil in a small saucepan. Cook, stirring constantly, until the mixture melts and thickens slightly, about 3 minutes; let cool. Refrigerate, covered, until ready to use.

**4.** To serve, invert the molds onto individual plates and peel off the cheesecloth. Serve with the apricot sauce and the mint sprigs.

Per serving (1 coeur à la crème with 3 tablespoons apricot sauce): 240 Cal, 2 g Fat, 1 g Sat Fat, 1 mg Chol, 238 mg Sod, 51 g Carb, 1 g Fib, 7 g Prot, 67 mg Calc. ***POINTS*** value: **5.**

life is sweet!

Berry Meringues with
Crème Anglaise

# Berry Meringues with Crème Anglaise

**MAKES 8 SERVINGS**

Meringues—light, delicious, and fat-free! What could be better? Here, they are topped with fresh berries and served with a light crème anglaise (custard sauce). For a change, top them with low-fat ice cream, frozen yogurt, or fresh fruit.

4 egg whites
$1/4$ teaspoon cream of tartar
$3/4$ cup + $1/3$ cup granulated sugar
$1^{3}/4$ cup low-fat (1%) milk
1 vanilla bean, halved lengthwise, or 1 teaspoon vanilla extract
3 egg yolks
1 cup fresh strawberries, hulled and sliced
1 cup fresh blueberries
1 cup fresh raspberries
Confectioners' sugar for dusting

1. Preheat the oven to 200°F. Line 2 large baking sheets with aluminum foil.

2. With an electric mixer on medium speed, beat the egg whites and cream of tartar in a large bowl until just frothy. Gradually sprinkle in $3/4$ cup of the granulated sugar, 2 tablespoons at a time, until sugar completely dissolves and the whites stand in stiff, glossy peaks, about 8 minutes.

3. Spoon the egg-white mixture onto the baking sheets, making 8 (6-inch) rounds. Spread the mixture with the back of a spoon or a small metal spatula, leaving about $1/2$ inch between each meringue.

4. Bake the meringues until they feel crisp to the touch, about 2 hours. Turn the oven off and leave the meringues in the oven until they are crisp and dry to the touch, about 1 hour longer.

5. Cool the meringues on the baking sheets on racks 10 minutes. Carefully loosen and transfer the meringues with a metal spatula to the racks to cool completely.

6. Meanwhile, to prepare the crème anglaise, bring the milk and vanilla bean to a boil in a medium saucepan; remove from heat. Remove the vanilla bean, scraping the fragrant seeds from inside the bean into the milk. If using vanilla extract, stir into the hot milk mixture off the heat.

*[continued on next page]*

life is sweet!

Berry Meringues with Crème Anglaise [*continued*]

**7.** Whisk the egg yolks and the remaining ⅓ cup granulated sugar in a bowl until the sugar is dissolved and the mixture is slightly thickened and a pale yellow. Whisk ½ cup of the hot milk mixture into the egg mixture. Slowly pour the egg mixture back into the hot milk mixture, whisking quickly and constantly. Cook over low heat, stirring constantly, until the mixture thickens and coats the back of a spoon, about 6 minutes. (Do not boil or the mixture may curdle.) Transfer the custard to a bowl; let cool. Refrigerate, covered, until chilled, at least 2 hours or up to 2 days.

**8.** To serve, combine the strawberries, blueberries, and raspberries in a bowl. Drizzle about 3 tablespoons of the crème anglaise onto each serving plate. Top each plate with a meringue, then about ⅓ cup of the berries and a sprinkling of confectioners' sugar.

Per serving (1 meringue, ⅓ cup berries, and 3 tablespoons crème anglaise): 184 Cal, 3 g Fat, 1 g Sat Fat, 82 mg Chol, 59 mg Sod, 36 g Carb, 2 g Fib, 5 g Prot, 83 mg Calc. *POINTS* value: *4.*

Humidity can play a factor in the meringues' crispness, so it's best not to make them on a rainy or humid day.

meals in minutes

# Blueberry Clafouti

**MAKES 8 SERVINGS**

Clafouti is a light, custard-like French dessert. It can be made with a variety of fresh fruits or berries. You can also substitute pitted ripe cherries, peaches, pears, or apples for the blueberries, if you prefer.

4 **cups fresh blueberries**
½ **cup low-fat (1%) milk**
½ **cup granulated sugar**
3 **tablespoons all-purpose flour**
2 **large eggs**
1 **tablespoon melted butter**
2 **teaspoons grated lemon zest**
½ **teaspoon ground cinnamon**
**Confectioners' sugar for dusting**

1. Preheat the oven to 375°F. Spray a shallow 2-quart baking dish with nonstick spray. Spoon the blueberries into the baking dish.

2. Process the milk, granulated sugar, flour, eggs, butter, lemon zest, and cinnamon in a food processor until smooth. Pour the batter over the berries.

3. Bake, uncovered, until the top is golden and a knife inserted into the center comes out clean, 35–40 minutes. Cool to room temperature on a rack, about 1 hour. Sprinkle with the confectioners' sugar just before serving.

Per serving (⅛ of clafouti): 139 Cal, 3 g Fat, 1 g Sat Fat, 58 mg Chol, 38 mg Sod, 26 g Carb, 2 g Fib, 3 g Prot, 32 mg Calc. **POINTS** value: **3**.

life is sweet!

# Lemon Curd Tartlets

**MAKES 8 SERVINGS**

Thick, rich, and tangy lemon curd makes a wonderful tart filling. You can also spread it between cake layers—or, for a fast but decadent snack, on graham crackers.

$^3/_4$ **cup sugar**

$^1/_2$ **cup fat-free egg substitute**

$^1/_3$ **cup + 2 tablespoons fresh lemon juice**

4 **tablespoons chilled unsalted butter**

1 **tablespoon cornstarch**

1 **teaspoon grated lemon zest**

8 **mini phyllo cups, at room temperature**

**1.** In a medium saucepan over medium-low heat, combine the sugar, egg substitute, and $^1/_3$ cup of the lemon juice. Cook, stirring constantly, until steaming, about 3 minutes. While stirring, add the butter, 1 tablespoon at a time, allowing it to melt completely between additions. Remove the saucepan from the heat.

**2.** In a small bowl, dissolve the cornstarch in remaining 2 tablespoons of lemon juice. Stir into the saucepan along with the lemon zest. Cook over medium heat until the mixture is bubbling and thick enough to coat the back of a spoon, about 10 minutes. Spoon 1 tablespoon of the lemon curd into each of the phyllo shells. Chill 1 hour before serving.

Per serving (1 tartlet): 175 Cal, 4 g Fat, 2 g Sat Fat, 8 mg Chol, 121 mg Sod, 31 g Carb, 0 g Fib, 4 g Prot, 14 mg Calc. **POINTS** value: **4.**

Allow the curd to cook for the full 10 minutes after adding the cornstarch, even if it appears to be done earlier. Cornstarch needs to cook until bubbling in order to thicken properly.

meals in minutes

# Raspberry Napoleons

**MAKES 6 SERVINGS**

Napoleons are not often included on lists of skinny desserts. But this one is—thanks to our replacing the usual butter-laden puff pastry layers with crisp phyllo. You can finish these gems with a dusting of confectioners' sugar or a drizzling of melted chocolate.

2 (12 x 17-inch) sheets phyllo, at room temperature

2 tablespoons + 2 teaspoons sugar

⅓ cup fat-free egg substitute

⅔ cup fat-free milk

½ tablespoon cornstarch

1 teaspoon vanilla extract

1 pint fresh raspberries

1. Preheat the oven to 400°F. Place 1 sheet of the phyllo on a work surface and spray with nonstick spray. Dust with 1 teaspoon of the sugar. Place the second sheet on top, spray it, and dust with another teaspoon of the sugar. Cut in half crosswise and position one half on top of the other to form an 8 x 12-inch rectangle. Cut into 12 (4 x 2-inch) pieces and transfer to a baking sheet. Bake until browned, 4–5 minutes. Cool in pan on a rack.

2. In a bowl, whisk the egg substitute and the remaining 2 tablespoons sugar. In a small saucepan, heat the milk over low heat until it begins to steam, 2–3 minutes. While whisking, drizzle the milk into the egg substitute mixture. Pour this mixture into the saucepan and cook over medium-low heat, stirring constantly, until just thick enough to coat the back of a spoon, 8–10 minutes. Dissolve cornstarch into the vanilla and add it to the milk mixture. Cook, stirring, until custard is very thick, 5–6 minutes longer.

3. Spread 2 tablespoons of custard on each of 6 phyllo rectangles. Divide the raspberries over the custard, then top each with a second phyllo rectangle.

Per serving (1 napoleon): 99 Cal, 2 g Fat, 0 g Sat Fat, 1 mg Chol, 95 mg Sod, 16 g Carb, 3 g Fib, 5 g Prot, 58 mg Calc. **POINTS** value: *2.*

COOK TO COOK

For a single large tart, bake the 8½ x 12-inch layered phyllo rectangle intact, without cutting it into pieces, then thinly spread with the custard and top with 2 pints of fresh raspberries.

life is sweet!

# Éclairs with Almond Cream

**MAKES 12 SERVINGS**

Éclairs are much easier to make than you think. You can even fill these with prepared sugar-free chocolate pudding or light whipped topping instead of making the cream.

**Cream-Puff Dough:**
- 1 cup water
- ¼ cup butter
- 1 teaspoon granulated sugar
- ⅛ teaspoon salt
- 1 cup all-purpose flour
- 1 large egg
- 2 egg whites

**Almond Cream:**
- ¼ cup granulated sugar
- 2 tablespoons all-purpose flour
- ½ teaspoon salt
- 1½ cups low-fat (1%) milk
- 1 large egg
- 1 teaspoon almond extract
- Confectioners' sugar for dusting

**1.** Preheat oven to 400°F. Lightly spray a large baking sheet with nonstick spray. Line the sheet with parchment paper.

**2.** Cream-puff dough: Bring the water, butter, sugar, and salt to a boil in a medium saucepan. Stir in the flour all at once; cook, stirring constantly with a wooden spoon, until dough begins to pull away from sides of pan, 1–2 minutes. Remove from heat and stir in the egg and egg whites, one at a time, beating vigorously after each, until dough is shiny and smooth. The dough will separate as you add the eggs; keep beating as it smooths out, stiffens, and holds its shape.

**3.** Spoon dough into a pastry bag fitted with a ½-inch plain tip. Pipe dough onto baking sheet into 12 (3½-inch) strips. Bake until golden, about 30 minutes. Let rest on baking sheet until cool enough to handle, 2–3 minutes, then split in half lengthwise with a sharp knife to allow the steam to escape. Remove and discard some of the soft dough from the centers. Cool éclairs completely on a rack.

**4.** Almond cream: Combine granulated sugar, flour, and salt in a medium saucepan. Whisk in milk and egg. Cook over medium-low heat, stirring constantly, until mixture coats the back of a spoon, about 8 minutes (do not boil). Remove from heat; stir in almond extract. Transfer to a small bowl.

**5.** Place the bowl into a larger bowl filled with ice cubes and water. Refrigerate, covered, until the mixture mounds when dropped from a spoon, about 30 minutes.

**6.** Spoon about 2 tablespoons of pastry cream into each éclair. Dust with confectioners' sugar and serve at once.

Per serving (1 éclair): 128 Cal, 5 g Fat, 3 g Sat Fat, 47 mg Chol, 133 mg Sod, 16 g Carb, 0 g Fib, 4 g Prot, 45 mg Calc. *POINTS* value: *3*.

Éclairs with
Almond Cream

# Ginger-Apple Tea Bread

**MAKES 10 SERVINGS**

This fruity bread remains wonderfully fresh and flavorful for up to one week. The sweet Fuji apples hold their shape well, but Jonathan, Gala, or Rome would be a good choice too. Select good-sized apples; you'll need about 1 cup chopped for the recipe.

2 Fuji apples, peeled and chopped (about 1 cup)
2 teaspoons fresh lemon juice
2 cups all-purpose flour
1 cup sugar
2 teaspoons baking powder
1¼ teaspoons ground ginger
¾ teaspoon ground cinnamon
½ teaspoon salt
1 large egg
1 cup fat-free milk
2 tablespoons vegetable oil

1. Preheat the oven to 375°F; lightly spray a 5 x 9-inch loaf pan with nonstick spray.

2. In a small bowl combine the apples and lemon juice. In a medium bowl whisk the flour, sugar, baking powder, ginger, cinnamon, and salt. In a large bowl, whisk the egg until frothy, then whisk in the milk and oil. Stir in the apples, then add the flour mixture and stir until just blended (do not overmix).

3. Pour into the loaf pan. Bake until the loaf is golden and a toothpick inserted into the center of the bread comes out clean, 55–60 minutes. Remove from the pan and cool on a wire rack.

Per serving (¹⁄₁₀ of loaf): 225 Cal, 4 g Fat, 0 g Sat Fat, 19 mg Chol, 182 mg Sod, 45 g Carb, 1 g Fib, 4 g Prot, 39 mg Calc. **POINTS** value: **5.**

# Fresh Peach Cake

**MAKES 12 SERVINGS**

You'll want to use the juiciest peaches you can find for this lovely dessert. If peaches are not in season, you can substitute 6 cups of thawed frozen sliced peaches. Just make sure to drain them well and pat dry with paper towels. Fresh nectarines, plums, and apricots also make an excellent choice.

2 ¼ cups reduced-fat baking mix

7 tablespoons sugar

²/₃ cup low-fat (1%) milk

3 tablespoons melted butter

8 (about 2 pounds) ripe peaches, pitted and sliced (6 cups)

³/₄ cup light nondairy whipped topping

**1.** Preheat the oven to 425°F. Spray an 8-inch-square cake pan with nonstick spray. Line the bottom of the cake pan with wax paper. Spray the wax paper with nonstick spray.

**2.** Combine the baking mix, 5 tablespoons of the sugar, the milk, and butter in a medium bowl until blended. Scrape the dough into the pan.

**3.** Bake until a toothpick inserted into the center comes out clean, 20–25 minutes. Cool the cake in the pan on a rack for 10 minutes; remove from the pan and cool completely on the rack.

**4.** Toss the peaches with the remaining 2 tablespoons sugar in a bowl until the sugar dissolves. Split the cooled cake in half horizontally. Place the bottom layer onto a cake plate; top with half of the peach mixture. Spoon the whipped topping over the peaches. Place the remaining cake layer on top. Spoon the remaining peaches into the center. Serve immediately.

Per serving (¹/₁₂ of cake): 177 Cal, 5 g Fat, 3 g Sat Fat, 8 mg Chol, 275 mg Sod, 30 g Carb, 2 g Fib, 3 g Prot, 42 mg Calc. *POINTS* value: *4.*

life is sweet!

Peaches-and-Cream Shortcakes

# Peaches-and-Cream Shortcakes

**MAKES 8 SERVINGS**

Shortcakes were originally more of a sponge cake, but buttermilk biscuits or baking powder biscuits are now commonly used. For variety, substitute 1 pint fresh blueberries, 1 pint fresh strawberries, or a mixture of berries for the peaches.

2 cups all-purpose flour

1 tablespoon baking powder

1 tablespoon grated orange zest

1 teaspoon chopped crystallized ginger

¼ teaspoon salt

1 cup low-fat buttermilk

3 peaches, thinly sliced

¼ cup granulated sugar

¾ cup fat-free evaporated milk, chilled

1½ tablespoons confectioners' sugar

1. Preheat the oven to 425°F.

2. In a large bowl, whisk the flour, baking powder, orange zest, ginger, and salt. Stir in the buttermilk to form a soft dough. With floured hands, knead the dough into a ball in the bowl, working in any excess flour. Transfer to a lightly floured surface and pat into a 7 x 8-inch rectangle about ½-inch thick. Using a biscuit cutter or glass, cut out 8 (2½-inch) rounds, pushing the dough scraps together for the last rounds if necessary. Place the rounds on a nonstick baking sheet and bake until lightly golden, about 12 minutes. Cool completely on a wire rack. Meanwhile, combine the peaches and granulated sugar in a bowl; let stand 15–20 minutes.

3. To make the whipped topping, pour the evaporated milk into a chilled bowl. With an electric mixer on high speed, beat until frothy. While mixing, slowly sprinkle with the confectioners' sugar; continue to beat until soft peaks form, about 3–4 minutes.

4. Split the biscuits open. Layer with the peaches, then dollop with the whipped topping.

Per serving (1 shortcake): 197 Cal, 1 g Fat, 0 g Sat Fat, 3 mg Chol, 219 mg Sod, 41 g Carb, 2 g Fib, 6 g Prot, 43 mg Calc. **POINTS** value: **4.**

**COOK TO COOK** Although you can't whip fat-free evaporated milk to be really firm, it's a great fake-out for softly whipped cream. For best results, put the bowl and the beaters in the freezer about 20 minutes before beating, and make sure the fat-free evaporated milk is very well chilled.

life is sweet!

# Lemon Angel Food Cake

**MAKES 12 SERVINGS**

This delicate cake with a touch of citrus is delicious all on its own, but for a truly impressive dessert, spoon orange segments and raspberries on top.

2 cups sifted cake flour
12 egg whites
1¼ teaspoons cream of tartar
2 cups granulated sugar
1 tablespoon grated
 lemon zest
1 teaspoon lemon extract
Confectioners' sugar
 for dusting

1. Preheat the oven to 375°F. Sift the flour into a small bowl; set aside.

2. With an electric mixer on medium speed, beat the egg whites and cream of tartar in a large bowl until thick and foamy. Beat in the granulated sugar, 1 tablespoon at a time, until shiny, medium peaks form, 3–5 minutes.

3. With a large spatula, fold in the flour in 3 additions, gently folding each addition into the egg whites until well combined. Fold in the lemon zest and lemon extract.

4. Pour the batter into an ungreased 10-inch tube pan. Bake until the cake springs back when lightly touched, 35–40 minutes. Invert the cake in the pan onto its legs or onto the neck of a bottle; cool completely in the pan.

5. To serve, run a thin-bladed knife around edges of pan and center tube; invert onto a cake plate and sprinkle with the confectioners' sugar.

Per serving (¹⁄₁₂ of cake): 219 Cal, 0 g Fat, 0 g Sat Fat, 0 mg Chol, 56 mg Sod, 49 g Carb, 0 g Fib, 5 g Prot, 121 mg Calc. **POINTS** value: **4.**

Be sure to use a serrated knife when slicing the cake, wiping the blade with a damp towel each time you slice. The tube pan used to make this dessert should be absolutely clean and grease-free. Any residue in the pan will prevent the cake from rising properly.

meals in minutes

# Lemon-Glazed Tea Cake

**MAKES 12 SERVINGS**

If you glaze this cake while it's still warm, all the lemon-sugar syrup will soak into the cake. If you prefer a harder glaze, double the amount of lemon juice and sugar in Step 4; pour half on while the cake is warm and the remainder after both the cake and the syrup have cooled. You can also dust the glazed cake with a bit of confectioners' sugar.

1 cup + 6 tablespoons sugar
1 cup cake flour
1 teaspoon baking powder
¼ teaspoon salt
⅓ cup fat-free egg substitute
2 tablespoons canola oil
1 egg yolk
4 teaspoons grated lemon zest
1 teaspoon vanilla extract
5 egg whites, at room temperature
¼ cup fresh lemon juice

**1.** Preheat the oven to 350°F; spray a 10-inch Bundt pan with nonstick spray.

**2.** Sift ¾ cup of the sugar, the flour, baking powder, and salt into a large bowl. Whisk in the egg substitute, oil, egg yolk, lemon zest, and vanilla until smoothly blended.

**3.** In another bowl, with electric mixer on medium-high speed, beat the egg whites until thick. While mixing, gradually add ¼ cup of the sugar. Beat until stiff, glossy peaks form. With a rubber spatula, fold about one-third of the meringue into the flour mixture. Stir well, then fold in the remainder of the meringue. Pour into the pan. Bake until a toothpick inserted into the center comes out clean, about 30 minutes. Cool in the pan on a rack 10 minutes, then unmold the cake onto the rack.

**4.** In a small saucepan over medium heat, combine the lemon juice and the remaining 6 tablespoons sugar. Cook, stirring constantly, until the sugar dissolves completely, about 2 minutes. Pour over the cake and allow to cool completely before serving.

Per serving (¹⁄₁₂ of cake): 158 Cal, 3 g Fat, 0 g Sat Fat, 18 mg Chol, 104 mg Sod, 30 g Carb, 0 g Fib, 3 g Prot, 9 mg Calc. **POINTS** value: **3.**

life is sweet!

When you glaze the cake, place a sheet of foil under the cooling rack to catch the syrup. Pour any syrup that drips onto the foil back over the cake.

# Chocolate Bread Pudding

**MAKES 12 SERVINGS**

Chocolate lovers will rave about this homey bread pudding. The recipe calls for Dutch process cocoa powder, which is richer and darker than its regular counterpart. If you can't find challah, substitute another sweet egg bread.

⅓ cup boiling water

3 tablespoons unsweetened Dutch process cocoa powder

1 tablespoon light corn syrup

2 (12-ounce) cans fat-free evaporated milk

1 cup packed light brown sugar

½ cup fat-free egg substitute

2 large eggs

2 teaspoons vanilla extract

6 cups cubed challah bread (about ½ loaf)

1. In a small bowl, combine the boiling water, cocoa, and corn syrup. In a large bowl, whisk together the evaporated milk, brown sugar, egg substitute, eggs, and vanilla. Whisk in the cocoa mixture, then stir in the bread cubes. Let stand until the bread absorbs some of the liquid and softens slightly, about 30 minutes.

2. Preheat the oven to 350°F. Pour the mixture into a 5 x 9-inch loaf pan. Place the loaf pan inside a larger baking dish on the middle oven rack. Pour enough hot water into the baking dish to come halfway up the sides of the loaf pan. Bake until the pudding is set and knife inserted into the center comes out clean, 55–65 minutes. Cool the pudding in the pan on a wire rack. Serve at room temperature or chilled.

Per serving (¹/₁₂ of pudding): 203 Cal, 2 g Fat, 1 g Sat Fat, 46 mg Chol, 200 mg Sod, 35 g Carb, 1 g Fib, 8 g Prot, 44 mg Calc. **POINTS** value: **4.**

meals in minutes

# Banana Crème Caramel

**MAKES 16 SERVINGS**

This is a showstopper party dish, whether you're hosting or bringing a dessert. Since it needs to chill for several hours, it's a make-ahead (up to a day in advance). The longer it sits, the more the caramel topping will liquefy and take on a sauce-like consistency.

2 cups mashed ripe bananas (about 5 bananas)
1 (14-ounce) can fat-free sweetened condensed milk
1 (12-ounce) can fat-free evaporated milk
1 cup fat-free egg substitute
1/3 cup golden rum
1 large egg
1/2 tablespoon vanilla extract
1 cup sugar
3 tablespoons water

1. Preheat the oven to 325°F.

2. In a large bowl combine the bananas, condensed milk, evaporated milk, egg substitute, rum, egg, and vanilla; whisk until blended and frothy.

3. In a small heavy-bottomed saucepan combine the sugar and water over high heat. Cook, stirring constantly, until the sugar dissolves, 1–2 minutes. Reduce the heat to medium and cook, swirling the pan occasionally (do not stir), until the mixture has become a very thin liquid and is a deep caramel brown, 7–10 minutes. Pour the caramel syrup into 2 (4-cup) glass bowls or soufflé dishes, swirling to coat the bottoms and partway up the sides. Pour the banana mixture into the bowls.

4. Put the bowls into a large baking dish; add enough hot water to the baking dish to come halfway up the sides of the bowls. Bake until the custards are set and a knife inserted into the center of a custard comes out clean, about 1½ hours. Cool on a rack, then refrigerate, covered, until thoroughly chilled, at least 4 hours.

5. To serve, invert custards onto platters, letting caramel syrup pool around custard. Cut each into 8 servings.

Per serving (⅛ of 1 custard): 219 Cal, 1 g Fat, 0 g Sat Fat, 50 mg Chol, 201 mg Sod, 79 g Carb, 1 g Fib, 14 g Prot, 213 mg Calc. **POINTS** value: **4.**

Sugar syrup can be very temperamental; once the sugar dissolves, take care not to stir the syrup lest it seizes up on you. And be very careful when you are pouring the caramel syrup into the bowls. Because the syrup is so sticky, it can result in a painful burn if it gets on your skin.

# Hot Lemon and Raspberry Soufflé

## MAKES 6 SERVINGS

Individual hot lemon soufflés with a raspberry surprise on the bottom make a light and refreshing finish to any meal. If you don't own soufflé molds, use 6-ounce custard cups.

2 tablespoons + ⅓ cup
  granulated sugar
¼ cup seedless
  raspberry jam
1 tablespoon butter
3 tablespoons all-purpose
  flour
⅔ cup low-fat (1%) milk
1 tablespoon grated
  lemon zest
½ cup fresh lemon juice
2 egg yolks
4 egg whites
Confectioners' sugar
  for dusting

1. Preheat the oven to 400°F. Spray 6 (6-ounce) soufflé molds with nonstick spray. Sprinkle 2 tablespoons of the granulated sugar into one of the molds, turning constantly, so bottom and sides are coated. Toss sugar remaining in the mold into the next mold, and repeat until all molds are coated. Spoon 1 teaspoon raspberry jam into bottom of each mold. Refrigerate the molds until ready to use.

2. Melt the butter in a small nonstick saucepan over low heat. Sprinkle in the flour and whisk until smooth. Cook, stirring constantly, 1 minute. Whisk in the milk and bring to a boil, whisking constantly. Remove from heat and transfer milk mixture to a bowl. Stir in the lemon zest and juice. Stir in the egg yolks, one at a time, until blended.

3. With an electric mixer on medium speed, beat the egg whites in medium bowl until soft peaks form, 2–3 minutes. Sprinkle in the remaining ⅓ cup granulated sugar and beat until stiff, glossy peaks form, about 3 minutes. Stir about one-quarter of the beaten egg whites into the milk mixture to lighten. Gently fold in remaining egg whites.

4. Spoon the batter into the soufflé molds, filling each about three-quarters full. Arrange molds in a roasting pan lined with paper towels to prevent them from slipping. Place the pan in the oven, then carefully fill the roasting pan with hot water until it reaches two-thirds up the sides of the soufflé molds. Bake until golden brown and puffed, about 25 minutes. Carefully remove soufflés from the water bath. Dust with confectioners' sugar and serve at once.

Per serving (1 soufflé): 170 Cal, 4 g Fat, 2 g Sat Fat, 77 mg Chol,
76 mg Sod, 30 g Carb, 0 g Fib, 5 g Prot, 49 mg Calc. **POINTS** value: **4.**

Hot Lemon
and Raspberry
Soufflé

# New York–Style Strawberry Cheesecake

**MAKES 16 SERVINGS**

New York cheesecake is famous for its ultra-rich taste and texture, and this light version is no exception. The recipe successfully cuts the fat by using nonstick spray in lieu of butter to make a graham cracker crust.

- ¼ **cup fine graham cracker crumbs**
- 2 **(8-ounce) packages light cream cheese (Neufchâtel)**
- 2 **(8-ounce) packages fat-free cream cheese**
- 1 **cup sugar**
- 3 **tablespoons all-purpose flour**
- 1½ **cups fat-free egg substitute**
- 1 **tablespoon vanilla extract**
- 1 **teaspoon grated lemon zest**
- 3 **tablespoons currant jelly, melted**
- 1 **quart fresh strawberries, hulled**

**1.** Preheat the oven to 350°F; spray the inside of a 9-inch springform pan with nonstick spray and dust with the graham cracker crumbs.

**2.** In a large bowl, with an electric mixer on medium speed, beat both kinds of cheese, the sugar, and flour until well blended. While mixing, drizzle in the egg substitute. Continue to beat until light and fluffy. Mix in the vanilla and lemon zest. Pour into the pan. Bake until the cake is golden and firm to the touch and a tester inserted into the center comes out clean, about 1 hour. Cool completely in the pan on a wire rack 2–3 hours, then cover with foil and refrigerate at least 1 hour or until ready to serve.

**3.** Lightly brush the top of the cake with the melted jelly. Place the strawberries on top, hulled-side down, then drizzle with the remainder of the jelly.

Per serving (¹/₁₆ of cheesecake): 212 Cal, 8 g Fat, 5 g Sat Fat, 24 mg Chol, 322 mg Sod, 25 g Carb, 2 g Fib, 11 g Prot, 95 mg Calc. **POINTS** value: **5.**

Be sure to let the cake cool completely in the pan. If you release the springform pan's clamp too soon, the cake may fall.

# Raspberry Cheesecake

**MAKES 12 SERVINGS**

This rich and creamy cheesecake tastes remarkably like the full-fat version. Don't worry if your cake cracks: Cracking is characteristic of cheesecakes after they are baked, especially when using fat-free ingredients. However, spooning fresh berries on top hides the cracking and presents beautifully. This cheesecake is better made one or even two days ahead and kept in the refrigerator. Top with the raspberries just before serving.

10 reduced-fat cinnamon graham crackers
2 tablespoons applesauce
1 tablespoon melted butter
4 (8-ounce) packages fat-free cream cheese
1¼ cups granulated sugar
1 cup fat-free egg substitute
1 tablespoon fresh lemon juice
1 teaspoon vanilla extract
1 pint fresh raspberries
Confectioners' sugar for dusting

1. Preheat the oven to 350°F. Spray a 9-inch springform pan with nonstick spray.

2. Place the graham crackers in a large zip-close plastic bag. Crush the crackers with a rolling pin until fine crumbs form. Transfer the crumbs to a bowl. Stir in the applesauce and butter until blended. Scatter the crumb mixture evenly over the bottom of the pan. Refrigerate the pan until ready to use.

3. With an electric mixer on medium speed, beat the cream cheese in a large bowl until smooth. Gradually beat in the granulated sugar until well blended. Beat in the egg substitute, lemon juice, and vanilla until combined. Pour the filling evenly onto the crust.

4. Bake the cheesecake until a knife inserted into the center comes out clean, 45–50 minutes. Cool completely on a rack. Refrigerate, covered, at least 12 hours or up to 3 days before serving.

5. Remove the sides of the pan. Top the cheesecake with the raspberries, and sprinkle with confectioners' sugar just before serving.

Per serving (¹/₁₂ of cheesecake): 218 Cal, 2 g Fat, 1 g Sat Fat, 4 mg Chol, 462 mg Sod, 36 g Carb, 2 g Fib, 13 g Prot, 94 mg Calc.
***POINTS*** value: *4.*

life is sweet!

# Classic Chocolate Mousse

**MAKES 12 SERVINGS**

There's practically nothing but chocolate in this recipe, so use the best quality possible. Substitute semisweet or milk chocolate, according to your taste. Serve the mousse on dessert plates or in goblets or other pretty stemmed glasses, garnished with fresh fruit.

8 ounces bittersweet
   chocolate, melted
3 tablespoons orange
   liqueur
2 tablespoons light
   corn syrup
¼ cup powdered egg whites
¾ cup warm water
½ cup sugar

**1.** In a large bowl mix the chocolate, liqueur, and corn syrup. In another large bowl combine the powdered egg whites and warm water, stirring until the powder dissolves completely, about 2 minutes. With an electric mixer on low speed, beat until foamy; increase the speed to medium and beat until soft peaks form. While mixing, slowly add the sugar. Increase the speed to medium-high and continue beating until stiff, glossy peaks form.

**2.** With a rubber spatula, stir about one-third of the meringue into the chocolate mixture. Stir well, then fold in another third of the meringue. Gently fold in the remaining meringue until completely blended. Refrigerate the mousse, covered, until firm, at least 3 hours.

Per serving (¹/₁₂ of mousse): 150 Cal, 6 g Fat, 4 g Sat Fat, 1 mg Chol, 29 mg Sod, 21 g Carb, 1 g Fib, 3 g Prot, 11 mg Calc. **POINTS** value: **3.**

To melt the chocolate, microwave the chopped chocolate on Medium for about 4 minutes, stirring every minute. If you microwave it in a large bowl, you'll have one less dish to wash.

meals in minutes

# the scoop on sugar

along with the energy they provide, different types of sugar add to the enjoyment of eating and to the flavor of foods. In addition, sugars play an important role in food preparation. Some act as a preservative, while others provide texture. And when used in baking, sugar promotes a brown and flavorful crust. Of course, you should try to satisfy a sweet tooth with sugars that occur naturally in foods like fruits and low-fat dairy products. They contain important nutrients like calcium and soluble fiber, which can help curb your appetite. But sometimes, processed sweeteners are called for. So here's how some popular ones stack up when it comes to cooking and tasting.

**BROWN SUGAR** is sugar crystals that have been coated in molasses syrup. It's sold in two shades: dark and light. The dark variety has a stronger molasses flavor than the lighter version.

**CONFECTIONERS' SUGAR** is granulated sugar that has been ground to a smooth powder and then sifted. Also called powdered sugar, it's often used to make frosting and candy, as well as to decoratively dust desserts.

**GRANULATED SUGAR** is also known as table sugar, white sugar, or sucrose. It comes from sugar cane or the root of the sugar beet and is dried into crystals. It's the most common sweetener used in cooking and on the table.

**HONEY** is a sweetener produced by bees from the nectar of flowers. It contains slightly more calories than table sugar, but it's sweeter so you can use less. Bear in mind that darker honeys have stronger flavors than lighter ones.

**MOLASSES** is the thick syrup that's left when sugar cane juice evaporates during the production of table sugar. Its distinct dark color and bold flavor makes it just right for such desserts as gingerbread and Indian pudding.

life is sweet!

# about our recipes

We make every effort to ensure that you will have success with our recipes. For best results and for nutritional accuracy, please keep the following guidelines in mind:

★ All recipes feature approximate nutritional information; our recipes are analyzed for Calories (Cal), Total Fat (Fat), Saturated Fat (Sat Fat), Cholesterol (Chol), Sodium (Sod), Carbohydrates (Carb), Dietary Fiber (Fib), Protein (Prot), and Calcium (Calc).

★ Nutritional information for recipes that include meat, fish, and poultry are based on cooked skinless boneless portions (unless otherwise stated), with the fat trimmed as specified in the recipe.

★ All recipes include *POINTS* values based on the Weight Watchers weight-loss plan. *POINTS* values are calculated from a proprietary formula that takes into account calories, total fat, and dietary fiber.

★ Before serving, divide foods—including any vegetables, sauce, or accompaniments—into portions of equal size according to the designated number of servings per recipe.

★ Any substitutions made to the ingredients will alter the "Per serving" nutritional information and may affect the *POINTS* value.

★ Additionally, substituting fat-free foods for any low-fat ingredients specified in a recipe may affect the consistency, texture, or flavor of the finished dish.

★ If you prefer to avoid using alcohol in any recipe, you may substitute an equal amount of water, broth, or juice.

★ It is implied that all greens in recipes should be washed or rinsed.

★ All herbs called for are fresh, not dried, unless otherwise specified.

# dry and liquid measurement equivalents

If you are converting the recipes in this book to metric measurements, use the following chart as a guide.

Note: Measurement of less than ⅛ teaspoon is a dash or a pinch. Metric volume measurements are approximate.

| TEASPOONS | TABLESPOONS | CUPS | FLUID OUNCES |
|---|---|---|---|
| 3 teaspoons | 1 tablespoon | | ½ fluid ounce |
| 6 teaspoons | 2 tablespoons | ⅛ cup | 1 fluid ounce |
| 8 teaspoons | 2 tablespoons plus 2 teaspoons | ⅙ cup | |
| 12 teaspoons | 4 tablespoons | ¼ cup | 2 fluid ounces |
| 15 teaspoons | 5 tablespoons | ⅓ cup minus 1 teaspoon | |
| 16 teaspoons | 5 tablespoons plus 1 teaspoon | ⅓ cup | |
| 18 teaspoons | 6 tablespoons | ¼ cup plus 2 tablespoons | 3 fluid ounces |
| 24 teaspoons | 8 tablespoons | ½ cup | 4 fluid ounces |
| 30 teaspoons | 10 tablespoons | ½ cup plus 2 tablespoons | 5 fluid ounces |
| 32 teaspoons | 10 tablespoons plus 2 teaspoons | ⅔ cup | |
| 36 teaspoons | 12 tablespoons | ¾ cup | 6 fluid ounces |
| 42 teaspoons | 14 tablespoons | 1 cup minus 1 tablespoon | 7 fluid ounces |
| 45 teaspoons | 15 tablespoons | 1 cup minus 1 tablespoon | |
| 48 teaspoons | 16 tablespoons | 1 cup | 8 fluid ounces |

| VOLUME | |
|---|---|
| ¼ teaspoon | 1 milliliter |
| ½ teaspoon | 2 milliliters |
| 1 teaspoon | 5 milliliters |
| 1 tablespoon | 15 milliliters |
| 2 tablespoons | 30 milliliters |
| 3 tablespoons | 45 milliliters |
| ¼ cup | 60 milliliters |
| ⅓ cup | 80 milliliters |
| ½ cup | 120 milliliters |
| ⅔ cup | 160 milliliters |
| ¾ cup | 175 milliliters |
| 1 cup | 240 milliliters |
| 1 quart | 950 milliliters |

| OVEN TEMPERATURE | |
|---|---|
| 250°F | 120°C |
| 275°F | 140°C |
| 300°F | 150°C |
| 325°F | 160°C |
| 350°F | 180°C |
| 375°F | 190°C |
| 400°F | 200°C |
| 425°F | 220°C |
| 450°F | 230°C |
| 475°F | 250°C |
| 500°F | 260°C |
| 525°F | 270°C |

| WEIGHT | |
|---|---|
| 1 ounce | 30 grams |
| ¼ pound | 120 grams |
| ½ pound | 240 grams |
| ¾ pound | 360 grams |
| 1 pound | 480 grams |

| LENGTH | |
|---|---|
| 1 inch | 25 millimeters |
| 1 inch | 2.5 centimeters |

# index

meals in minutes

*index*

## D

index

index

# notes

# notes

meals in minutes

notes

# notes

meals in minutes

# Taco Casserole

1 (8 oz) Cornbread stuffing mix
1 (14 3/4 oz) can cream style corn
1 c water divided
1 1/2 lbs ground sirloin
1/2 c chopped onion
1 (15 oz) can black beans, drain
2/3 c Salsa    1 envelope Taco Seasoning
1 (8 oz) pkg shredded reduced-fat
          Mexican cheese

Preheat oven to 375°. Combine stuffing mix, corn + 1/2 c water stir well. Press into 13 X 9 sprayed dish. Bake 10 min. Remove + set aside. Cook meat + onions in large skillet till meat is brown. Drain, return to pan. Add other 1/2 c water, beans, salsa + taco seasoning. Stir well. Spoon over stuffing mixture. Top with cheese. Cover + bake 20 min or until cheese is bubbly. Cut into 12 servings.
1 serving = 6 points